THE TIMOTHY INITIATIVE

Disciples Making Disciples - Level 3
USA Edition

3.11.2021

This book belongs to:

_____

"What you have heard from me in the presence of many witnesses entrust to faithful men who will be able to teach others also."

2 Timothy 2:2

TTI Contact Information:

ttiusa@ttionline.org

TTI USA Website:

usa.ttionline.org

DMD Level 3 (USA Edition)
This edition published by The Timothy Initiative

For information:
The Timothy Initiative
P.O. Box 98177
Raleigh, NC 27624

All rights reserved.
Published and Printed in the United States of America.
Library of Congress Cataloging-in-Publication Data
Scripture quotations are from: The New King James Version
Copyright © 1979, 1980, 1982 by Thomas Nelson, Inc.

Acknowledgements

We deeply appreciate and honor the countless TTI church planters and disciple makers around the world. Your faithfulness, commitment, and hard work are an inspiration to all and have been a key ingredient in creating this manual.

Additionally, we would like to appreciate the editorial team who contributed directly to this edition: Fregy John, Moses Liancuh, Koudjoga Nenonene, Solomon Yero, Jared Nelms, Andre Harriott, Mario Kasih, Matt Tumas, Samuel Selvamony, David Nelms, Kasey Channita, Kevin Marsico, Matt Tumas, Reji Dineep, Krishna Ghimire, Daniel Boro, and many others. We appreciate Lanie McKenna's assistance and formatting efforts as well.

We also acknowledge and thank the following individuals and ministries for their godly character, leadership, insight, and inspiration, which contributed to the formation of this manual:
- Dr. George Patterson
- Curtis Sergeant, Ying Kai, and *T4T*
- David Watson and *Discovery Bible Study* principles
- Todd Wilson's *More: Finding Your Personal Calling*

Table of Contents

Section 1
Welcome and Introduction 1
TTI's Training Strategy 6
Disciples Making Disciples – Levels 1 & 2 Review 10
Everyone Has the Potential to Lead a Movement 17
Chapter 1: Our First & Primary Calling 22
Chapter 2: Growing as a Christlike Leader 29

Section 2
Chapter 3: Introduction to the Bible 43
Chapter 4: Communicating God's Word in Small Groups 52
Chapter 5: Communicating God's Word in Medium Groups ... 59
Chapter 6: Communicating God's Word in Large Groups 64

Section 3
Chapter 7: The Story of the Bible: God's Word to Humanity 70
Chapter 8: The Story of the Old Testament 77
Chapter 9: The Story of the New Testament 90

Section 4
Chapter 10: The Life and Ministry of Jesus 95
Chapter 11: The Story of the Church 112
Chapter 12: The Persecuted Church throughout History 130

Section 5
Chapter 13: Fulfilling the Great Commission 141
Chapter 14: Essentials of the Faith 150
Chapter 15: Defending Your Faith with Confidence 162
Chapter 16: Understanding Major World Religions 176
Chapter 17: Spiritual Warfare 183
Chapter 18: Marriage & Family 190

Conclusion: Your Investment 207
Appendix 209

Welcome and Introduction

Welcome to Disciples Making Disciples - Level 3

The purpose of this training manual is to equip disciples who will make disciples. We expect that by going through this manual:

- You will be equipped and actively share your faith with others. The Gospel will spread at a fast pace! The Kingdom of God will be expanded!
- You will be trained in the essentials of the Christian faith.
- You will make healthy disciples who make disciples.
- You will plant healthy churches that plant churches.

This training is not limited to you alone! God expects you to make disciples *(2 Timothy 2:2)*. Every training you receive is also a training you can give to others. You can use the tools and principles from this book to raise up future generations of disciple makers.

What is the Mission of TTI?

TTI's mission is to see reproducing, multiplying, church planting movements. In partnership with other national movement leaders, TTI desires to penetrate the nations and cultures with the Gospel of Jesus Christ.

TTI USA is an extension of The Timothy Initiative which has the goal of equipping pastors, church planters, and disciples to launch disciple making and micro-church planting movements in their towns, cities, and communities. We are all partners in the Great Commission and it is our main goal to see more lives transformed by the Gospel of Jesus Christ.

What are the Core Values of TTI?

1. **Kingdom-Focused:** It's all about the King of kings and His Kingdom, so we share the work and give God the credit.

2. **Spirit-Led – Scripture-Based:** The Holy Spirit and the Holy Scriptures are our guides in planting multiplying churches.

3. **Integrity First:** God values integrity ... so do we.

4. **Disciple Making Leads to Church Planting:** The best way to plant churches is by making disciple makers.

5. **Prayer Is Priority:** We pray throughout the process of planning and planting churches.

6. **People Matter:** All people matter to God, so we reach out to everyone—large and small tribes, people groups, urban cities, remote villages, rich, poor ... everyone!

7. **Faith-Driven:** We want to bring glory to God. If there is no faith involved, there is no glory for God.

Purpose and Expected Outcomes

The purpose and expected outcomes from this manual center on equipping disciples to make disciples and plant churches. In doing so, the Gospel will rapidly spread as more people begin to follow Jesus.

Chapter 1: Every disciple maker will understand they are called by God, to be with God and bear fruit as they live for God.

Chapter 2: Every disciple maker will intentionally grow as a Christlike leader while they equip others to do the same.

Chapter 3: Every disciple maker will see how God's Word is trustworthy and learn to interpret it accurately.

Chapter 4-6: Every disciple maker will lead Group Discovery Bible Studies and practice communicating the Bible in their group.

Chapter 7: As every disciple maker learns the story of the Bible, they will know the heart of God and be encouraged to faithfully follow His instruction.

Chapter 8: Every disciple maker will learn and share the story of the Old Testament.

Chapter 9: Every disciple maker will learn and share the story of the New Testament.

Chapter 10: Every disciple maker will model their life and ministry after the life and ministry of Jesus.

Chapter 11: Every disciple maker will model the way they make disciples and plant churches after the example of the early church.

Chapter 12: As every disciple maker shares Jesus boldly, they will be prepared and encouraged to faithfully respond to suffering and persecution with perseverance.

Chapter 13: Every disciple maker will be actively engaged in fulfilling the Great Commission.

Chapter 14: Every disciple maker will base their beliefs and worldview on a proper view of God and His Word by learning the essential beliefs of the Christian faith from God's Word.

Chapter 15: Every disciple maker will defend their faith with confidence based on the authority and accuracy of the Word of God.

Chapter 16: Every disciple maker will intentionally develop God-honoring relationships with those who practice other religions.

Chapter 17: Every disciple maker will be prepared for spiritual battle against the world, the devil, and their old human nature.

Chapter 18: Every disciple maker will love their spouse and intentionally disciple their family to be more like Jesus each and every day.

What is Our Definition of a Church?

For TTI, a church is this: **A group of believers under the authority of biblically qualified leadership, who meet together regularly to worship the Father, study, and communicate the Word of God in the power of the Holy Spirit. This group prays and fellowships together, observes the ordinances, and goes out to share the love of Christ to the lost world as they intentionally multiply disciples.**

A church can meet in a building, in a house, in a park, or anywhere! We suggest (for the sake of consistency) that every church reported have at least three unrelated individuals/families.

Biblically Qualified Leadership
Identify and remain accountable to local authority.

Gather Together Regularly
Establish a time and place to meet regularly.

Worship God, Pray, Fellowship & Discover the Word of God in the power of the Holy Spirit
When you gather, discover the Bible together, allowing time for worship, prayer, fellowship, giving, and commitment to being led by the Word and Spirit of God.

Observe the Ordinances
Consistently follow public declarations of salvation with baptism and remember Christ through communion.

Go out sharing the love of Christ to the world
Each gathering serves as a time to align and encourage disciples to the mission of the Great Commission and the ministry of reconciliation.

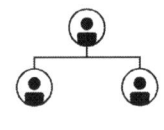

Intentionally multiply disciples
Every believer is a disciple and every disciple is expected and held accountable to be disciple makers.

TTI's Philosophy and Strategy of Training

Philosophy

TTI believes learning and doing go together. Both should lead to training others who can then go on to train others. Likewise, obedience is a critical part of discipleship; they should not be separated.

With this in mind, all of the training materials produced by TTI are not merely for educational purposes; every disciple maker is expected to put into practice what they learn in their personal life and ministry. As we partner together under the leading and direction of the Holy Spirit, He will provide each of us with everything we need to bring Him glory and the lost to His Son, Jesus!

TTI partners with churches and leaders to start disciple making Training Centers. Typically, training happens either in existing church buildings or in homes where participants receive hands-on training on how to make disciples of Jesus, who will in turn make more disciples of Jesus. All assignments center on spiritual growth, evangelism, and disciple making. For those interested, Disciples Making Disciples - Level 2 offers additional training on establishing micro-churches.

Strategy

Train disciple makers to make disciples where they live, work, study, shop, and play. In this manual, every disciple maker is encouraged to immediately start meeting with and intentionally developing any new believer they lead to Christ. They are also encouraged to target believers whom they know are not making disciples.

- The training is Christ-centered and Bible-based.
- The training is relational and non-formal (mentoring).
- The training is intentional, simple, and reproducible.

- The training is often held in a local church or home.
- The training is obedience-based and can be applied immediately to the disciple maker's life.

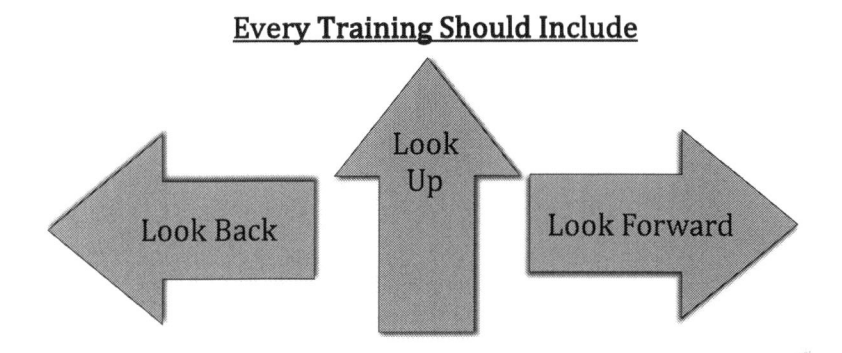

Every Training Should Include

Look Back ← **Look Up** ↑ **Look Forward** →

1. **Looking Back** gives everyone a chance to share about and listen to what is happening in their lives. This provides an opportunity for encouragement, celebration, and accountability. Looking back also allows challenges to be identified, course corrections to be made, and progress to be measured. Finally, it provides a chance to connect back to the core values, mission, vision, and purpose of the training.

2. **Looking Up** refuels our passion for loving God and others. Spending time in prayer and in God's Word provides nourishment to our souls and inspiration to continue forward. This offers a chance for each disciple maker to continue to learn and grow as Christlike leaders. Ministry is fueled by our relationship with God. Ownership of the core values, mission, and vision will only happen if we remain connected in relationship with Jesus.

   Hearing from God and responding to His Word is the primary aim of looking up. After each lesson has been taught, allow some time for prayer and reflection for each person to identify exactly what God is calling them to do. A simple way to do this is to invite God to speak to your heart and ask Him to show you the areas of greater obedience to which He is calling you.

3. **Looking Forward** offers a clear plan of action with timelines and expectations of what to do next. The next steps will be summarized with **"I will" statements** that bring clarity to what needs to be done before the next training. These next steps are based on what each person hears from God, what God is calling them to do, and how they can put it into action this week. There should be a strong commitment to following through and staying accountable throughout the process. Each trainer should make a note of the commitments made and hold all accountable.

Following the example of Looking Back, Looking Up, and Looking Forward will ensure that every training accomplishes the specific purposes, goals, and outcomes designed. This simple group structure, with this training material and a good trainer, will help every disciple maker grow in their **Beliefs, Skills, and Values.**

Beliefs, Skills, and Values

As a disciple and disciple maker, there are essential beliefs, skills, and values we should understand and develop to help us grow and live as mature followers of Jesus. We can define this simply:

- **Beliefs**: The biblical principles and understandings that develop a firm foundation, leading to a Spirit-filled, faith-filled, and loving lifestyle.
- **Skills**: The habits, patterns, and lifestyle behaviors we develop that help us grow and live as mature disciples and disciple makers.
- **Values**: The heartbeat and desires that reflect a lifestyle of obedience as mature disciples and disciple makers.

Every chapter in this book is designed to help us grow in our understanding of Scripture and how to apply those truths to our life. The "I will" commitments, assignments, and Looking Back and Looking Forward hold us accountable to grow as disciples and disciple makers. A good trainer with comprehensive training materials, good practices, and a reproducible process will help us become mature disciples who can be disciple makers.

Disciples Making Disciples Levels 1 & 2 Review

In Disciples Making Disciples Level 1, you were asked to begin praying for and sharing with 30 people in the circles where you live, work, shop, and play. In Disciples Making Disciples Level 2, you were taught how to use the Four Fields system of evangelism and church planting to reach more people with the Gospel. You have likely identified your chosen field and begun to see the fruit of your faithfulness to be led by the Spirit.

As you begin to work through Disciples Making Disciples Level 3, it is essential that you continue to evaluate the work God is doing.

Take some time to review the questions below based on the progress you've seen since you started your training. What have you seen God accomplish in the time you've been untying and raising your sails? Who on your list of 30 people have you been able to lead to the Lord? Have you started to identify and train new disciples to be the next generation of disciple makers and church planters? Answer the following questions to measure the progress you've seen

1. What are the results from your chosen field?

   _____

   _____

2. How many disciples have you made? How many baptisms?

   _____

3. How many DBS groups have you started?

   _____

4. How many micro-churches have been planted?

   _____

5. Have you identified some faithful disciples to begin training? What are their names?

   _____

   _____

6. Have you identified any empty fields that need churches?

   _____

   _____

7. Has your church taken in or begun to care for any orphans or widows? Or identified any social injustice?

   _____

   _____

8. What other needs has your church met in the local community?

   _____

Church Planting Plan

Introduced in *Disciples Making Disciples - Level 2,* the Church Planting Plan provides the disciple maker with basic questions and information to consider when selecting a location to begin making disciples and planting churches. The key steps involved include the following: Know the soil, mobilize the seed sowers, scatter the seed, partner with the Holy Spirit, and commit to the harvest. **Always remember, the Spirit of God is the One who gives the increase.** Make sure you target the field He is directing you to!

Update your progress so far on your Church Planting Plan.

1. Name of your chosen place(s) of ministry or desired field?

2. How much space does your field cover? How many families/homes? Total population? Provide an estimation:

3. How many churches need to be planted so there is a church within walkable distance for everyone?

4. How many disciple makers are to be developed and leaders to be trained?

5. Have you identified any unengaged people groups in your area or those you feel the Lord drawing you to? List them:

6. What are the specific features and social networks of your chosen field?
   - Sub-cultures & Common Interests:
   - Languages Spoken:
   - Economic Level:
   - Openness to the Gospel:
   - Religious Backgrounds:

As you pray through and answers to all of these questions above, begin putting down some new plans (or continue where you are working) that outline specific goals and the practical next steps required in order to stay on track.

As you enter your new field, what needs to be done first?

What are some goals that could be accomplished in the first six months?

One-year Goals?

Two-year Goals?

Three-year Goals?

Building on Prior Work

Have you continued to pray daily through the list of 30 people you made in *Disciples Making Disciples - Level 1?* Have you shared your story and God's story with everyone? Do you need to update your list with new people who do not follow Jesus or are not walking closely with Him? As you begin this next phase of training, think about other people you would like to add to your list who you want to start praying for and sharing your story with. The following page also contains a table for you to begin tracking the people who may be more receptive to what you have to share.

My list I commit to praying for daily and sharing my story:

1. _____   16. _____
2. _____   17. _____
3. _____   18. _____
4. _____   19. _____
5. _____   20. _____
6. _____   21. _____
7. _____   22. _____
8. _____   23. _____
9. _____   24. _____
10. _____   25. _____
11. _____   26. _____
12. _____   27. _____
13. _____   28. _____
14. _____   29. _____
15. _____   30. _____

The following categories can be used to keep track of how many people are receptive or interested in hearing what you have to share. As you go and share with others, add their names below.

Open to Prayer	Open to My Story

Open to God's Story	Opens Home for Fellowship

Responds to Invitation to Trust Jesus	Wants to Be Baptized

Wants to Start a Group Discovery Bible Study	Wants to Be Trained to Be a Disciple Maker

Keys to Mentoring

As churches are planted in your chosen field, the top priority must remain making disciples who make disciples. This will require intentional mentoring every step of the way. The ultimate aim of your mentoring is to equip faithful men and women towards spiritual maturity and unity in the church.

Remember the following keys to mentoring and ask those you are mentoring to evaluate how you are as their mentor.

Keys to Mentoring		
	Yes	Not Yet
Model skills (be specific with each skill)		
Meet regularly		
Love and respect for one another		
Pray together and be a source of encouragement		
Listen carefully to what is said and unsaid		
Emphasize simple, loving, childlike obedience to Christ		
Hold accountable and help plan what to do next. Correct when needed		
Help strategize on short-term and long-term objectives		
Recommend studies that support personal development and deal with actual felt needs		
Help network with other leaders		

Everyone Has the Potential to Lead a Movement

"For it will be like a man going on a journey, who called his servants and entrusted to them his property. To one he gave five talents, to another two, to another one, to each according to his ability. Then he went away. He who had received the five talents went at once and traded with them, and he made five talents more. So also he who had the two talents made two talents more. But he who had received the one talent went and dug in the ground and hid his master's money. Now after a long time the master of those servants came and settled accounts with them. And he who had received the five talents came forward, bringing five talents more, saying, 'Master, you delivered to me five talents; here, I have made five talents more.' His master said to him, 'Well done, good and faithful servant. You have been faithful over a little; I will set you over much. Enter into the joy of your master.' And he also who had the two talents came forward, saying, 'Master, you delivered to me two talents; here, I have made two talents more.' His master said to him, 'Well done, good and faithful servant. You have been faithful over a little; I will set you over much. Enter into the joy of your master.' He also who had received the one talent came forward, saying, 'Master, I knew you to be a hard man, reaping where you did not sow, and gathering where you scattered no seed, so I was afraid, and I went and hid your talent in the ground. Here, you have what is yours.' But his master answered him, 'You wicked and slothful servant! You knew that I reap where I have not sown and gather where I scattered no seed? Then you ought to have invested my money with the bankers, and at my coming I should have received what was my own with interest. So take the talent from him and give it to him who has the ten talents. For to everyone who has will more be given, and he will have an abundance. But from the one who has not, even what he has will be taken away. And cast the worthless servant into the outer darkness. In that place there will be weeping and gnashing of teeth.'" Matthew 25:14-30

This parable clearly demonstrates that God holds us accountable for how we respond to the instructions and opportunities He gives us. Scripture teaches a principle that affects how we choose and develop leaders. The principle is this: **Those who are faithful in the little things will be faithful in bigger things** *(Luke 16:10; 19:17)*. God's expectation for every disciple maker is to faithfully steward what they have been given *(Matthew 10:8; Luke 12:48)*, apply what they learn, and train others to do the same *(2 Timothy 2:2)*.

> **Key Principle: Faithfully stewarding God's blessings and giftings is not an option but the expectation for every disciple maker** *(1 Corinthians 4:2)*.

Another principle found in this parable teaches us about our responsibility to fulfill the Great Commission. The servant who received one talent and buried it came to his master saying, *"I knew you to be a hard man, reaping where you did not sow, and gathering where you scattered no seed."* Fear was the reason the servant gave for hiding the talent in the ground. The master's response to the fearful servant was, *"You knew that I reap where I have not sown and gather where I scattered no seed?"*

If the master in this parable represents Jesus and the servant represents us, the expectation to spread the Gospel throughout the whole world is **our responsibility**. During His ministry on earth, Jesus spent His time in and around Israel. He never went to the ends of the earth with the Gospel; that was the command He gave to His disciples. Jesus told His followers to GO into all nations, preaching the Gospel, and making disciples who make disciples *(Matthew 28:19-20)*. Just like the master in the parable, Jesus expects to reap where He has not sown, and He expects to gather where He has scattered no seed. How will He accomplish this? **He has sent us! We are the ones called and expected to sow the Gospel seeds to the ends of the earth.**

Fear kept the servant in the parable from multiplying his talent, and fear is often what keeps us from sharing the Gospel and multiplying disciples. As disciples of Jesus, we have been tasked with spreading the Gospel to the ends of the earth. Jesus already said one chapter before *"this gospel of the kingdom will be proclaimed throughout the whole world as a testimony to all nations, and then the end will come" (Matthew 24:14)*. One day, the Master will return, and we must strive to be found faithful and fruitful.

The Parable of the Talents teaches that God is a wise investor. He invests most heavily in those who are most faithful. This does not mean we earn our righteousness or God's love by our behavior, but we do show our faith by our works *(James 2:14-26)*. The key to being faithful is to consistently hear from God, put what is heard or learned into practice, and then train others to do the same. When we consistently do these faithful and fruitful practices, we will be amazed by what God's favor will bring about in our lives. When we do as He instructed and live obedient to His commands, God's blessings will multiply the work and the Kingdom of God will reach the ends of the earth.

Group Discussion: Am I a wise investment? To determine this, discuss the following questions:

- Are you consistently hearing from God through His Word, prayer, etc.? If so, what is He saying?
- How are you applying and obeying what is learned into your own life? What fruit are you seeing as a result of your obedience to God's instruction?
- How consistently are you sharing with others and training them to do the same things you are doing?

These ideas about faithfulness can be illustrated best by looking at a 3-legged stool.

FAITHFUL	HYPOCRITICAL	SELFISH
KNOWING DOING SHARING	KNOWING DOING SHARING	KNOWING DOING SHARING

Faithful Stool has three even legs—equally focused on **Knowing, Doing, & Sharing.**
- The Faithful Stool has three even legs because when you put what you learn and know into practice, and train others to do the same, you are being faithful.

Hypocritical Stool has uneven legs—focused primarily on **Knowing & Sharing.**
- An uneven leg in **Doing** is called the Hypocritical Stool because you know what to do, and train others to do it, but you do not do it yourself.

Selfish Stool has uneven legs—focused primarily on **Knowing & Doing.**
- An uneven leg in **Sharing** is called the Selfish Stool because you know what to do and do it but do not train others.

As a disciple, it is critical to sit on a 3-legged stool with even legs. The foundation you build upon will directly impact how deep and wide the work will be able to go. Remember, faithful with little results in faithful with much. This is what we want in our own lives, and it is what we desire to see in the lives of those we train. **Be careful that your ministry does not grow larger than your faithfulness to God or your heart for God.**

Consider the following real-life example from a TTI leader in Asia.

Kumar is from a people group that is unreached with the

Gospel. His entire family followed other gods and had a negative view of Christians. One day, a church planter came to Kumar's village and shared the Gospel. Kumar initially rejected the Gospel, but after some time, God softened his heart and through an incredible miracle, Kumar accepted Christ. Soon after coming to Christ, Kumar became a Titus and then a Timothy. As a Timothy, Kumar faithfully shared his transformation story, God's story, and began making disciples in his village and the surrounding villages. As a result, many people came to Christ and Kumar successfully planted a church as a Timothy and was able to develop others to do the same.

In the next 2 years of training, Kumar became a Paul and effectively raised up Timothys in his training center to also plant churches in the surrounding villages. With such a great work growing and Kumar's faithfulness to keep the movement growing, Kumar became a Master Trainer and oversaw multiple Pauls, and even began working in an unreached people group. In 2020, Kumar is leading the work in a particular region in his country and is TTI's first official **Movement Leader** *(one who has trained from a Titus-Timothy-Paul-Master Trainer-Movement Leader).*

So far, Kumar and his ministry partners have seen more than 200 villages reached with the Gospel and hundreds of churches planted. As a Movement Leader, the aim for Kumar is to go from hundreds of villages reached to thousands! Kumar's story is what inspired the idea that **everyone has the potential to lead a movement** *of disciples and churches. Kumar's entire ministry training has only been with TTI. This story is shared to both challenge and inspire you! It is clear that faithfully applying biblical principles and practices with the empowerment of the Holy Spirit can produce a great revival of disciples making disciples.* **Everyone has the potential to lead a movement of disciples and churches.**

Chapter 1
Trainer's Guide

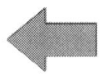

⬅ Look Back

Review the experiences and outcomes from Disciples Making Disciples - Levels 1 and 2.

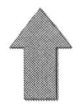

⬆ Look Up

This chapter introduces our first and primary calling: disciples of Jesus. It is critical that you focus on the following as you train through this chapter:

- Understand your identity is found in Jesus! This reminds us it is not based on what you do, where you come from, or anything related to your own efforts or abilities.
- Remember to highlight the **expected outcome** and **key principle**! Encourage memorization of key Scripture verses.
- **Hearing from God:** At the end of each chapter, allow for a time of silent prayer and reflection, specifically looking for what each person should do in response to God speaking to their heart.

Group Discussion: How do you feel about God's calling in your life and how it provides us with a new identity, purpose, and direction? How does your first and primary calling affect your daily life?

Model & Practice: Every trainer should demonstrate and model how they daily seek to share their story of Jesus changing their life. Review your list of names you are praying for, and if you need to make updates or changes, do so now. If you have not been keeping track, then begin a new list. Keep practicing, keep sharing, leave the results to God!

➡ Look Forward

Before moving on to the assignment for the week, ask the following questions:
- How is God speaking to your heart today?
- How is God calling you to greater obedience?
- What will you do today & this week in response to God's voice?

Assignment for this Chapter:
- Choose one of the Gospels to read/listen to this week (and the weeks to come). As you do, consider what behaviors or values need to change in your life in order to become more like Jesus. As you meditate on the Scripture, identify specific answers to the questions below.
    - What behaviors need to change in my life for me to become more like Jesus?
    - What values need to change in my life for me to become more like Jesus?
- Write "I will" statement(s) in the chapter journal.

Chapter 1
Our First & Primary Calling

Expected Outcome: Every disciple maker will understand they are called by God, to be with God and bear fruit as they live for God.

Scripture Reading: *John 15:1-17*

When was the last time you asked yourself the following questions?
- Who am I?
- Why do I do what I do?
- What matters most to me?

Our identity is normally connected back to our family or social background (tribe, language, people group, customs, traditions, culture, etc.). Many times, we find identity in what we do—being a pastor, a farmer, a businessperson, a parent, etc.

Consider for a moment: are there jobs/professions that your family, culture, or country values highly? Are there others that are looked down upon? Why is this the case? The answer is likely connected back to feelings of a greater status, meaning, or purpose.

No matter how great our accomplishments, without a connection back to a higher purpose, everything is meaningless. In today's world, there are many distractions. Some people have extra time but not enough money, while others feel they have money but not enough time. One thing that unites the world is a desire for meaning, purpose, and calling.

Calling gives clear understanding to our identity and purpose to our life. <u>We are not just called to something, but to</u>

<u>Someone—Jesus!</u> He said, *"Abide in me, and I in you ... By this my Father is glorified, that you bear much fruit and so prove to be my disciples" (John 15:4, 8).*

If there is no Caller, there is no calling—only meaningless work. Calling is not just about doing what we do or being who we are, it also includes becoming what we are called by God to be. The spiritual fruit that Jesus mentioned is an evidence of His life in us, and ultimately brings glory to God.

Abundant and fruitful living comes as a result of the condition of our heart, not as a result of our accomplishments. Jesus said, *"As the Father has loved me, so have I loved you. Abide in my love" (John 15:9).* Jesus tells us these things so that our joy may be complete *(John 15:11).* He also goes on to say how we are not only servants, but friends. We are friends by His choice!

Group Discussion: Take some time in prayer to reflect and meditate on the love of God. Read or listen to *John 15* and freely receive the love God has for you. Have you ever considered how to remain in God's love? As you pray, write down some thoughts that come to mind.

God calls us to Himself so strongly and so clearly that everything we are, everything we do, and everything we have is connected back to Him. We are called first and foremost to Someone—Jesus!

"Our primary calling as followers of Christ is by Him, to Him, and for Him." It is important to always remember that it is not our unique gifts that will change the world, it is the fullness of Jesus in us (being) and through us (doing). This gives our lives meaning and purpose and answers the question of why we do what we do.

Group Discussion: How do you feel about God's calling in your life and how it provides us with a new identity, purpose, and direction? Read the following passages and discuss what they reveal about your new identity in Christ.

Romans 8:10 _____

1 Corinthians 12:27 _____

1 Peter 2:9 _____

Galatians 3:26-28 _____

1 Thessalonians 5:4-5 _____

Ephesians 2:8-10 _____

Jesus' followers were known as the "called-out ones" (which is translated as church). In fact, the most common description of the disciples of Jesus was not Christians, but "followers of the Way" *(Acts 24:14).* **To be a disciple of Jesus is to be "a called-out one" by God, to God, and for God.** We are called and chosen to *"go and bear fruit and that your fruit should remain" (John 15:16).* **The fruit of being a disciple is to make disciples! We are called to be like Jesus.**

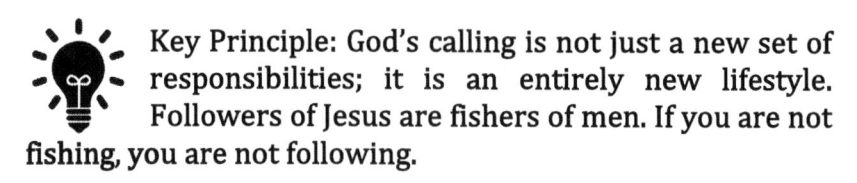

Key Principle: God's calling is not just a new set of responsibilities; it is an entirely new lifestyle. Followers of Jesus are fishers of men. If you are not fishing, you are not following.

God desires for us to live a life of obedience where circumstances and potential consequences of following Him do not distract us. **We must be aware of anything that challenges our loyalty to God.**

Model & Practice: Sharing Your Story
Take a moment to consider if there is any hesitation in your heart to trust God in any area of your life. Anything that

challenges our loyalty to God or takes the place of God in our life must be dealt with immediately. Remember, where your treasure is, there your heart will be *(Matthew 6:21)*. Every trainer will lead you through a time of prayer and reflection by going through the following questions.

Fill in the blank: I need to trust God more than I trust

_____.

- What are the obstacles in my life that are preventing me from becoming more like Jesus?
- What must be done today, without delay?
- Whom can I tell about these decisions?

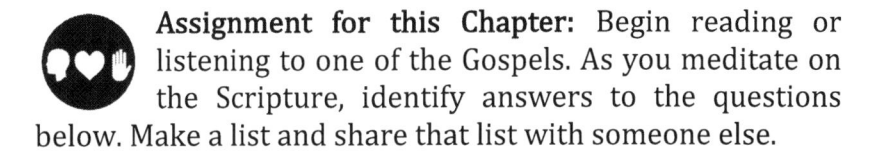

Assignment for this Chapter: Begin reading or listening to one of the Gospels. As you meditate on the Scripture, identify answers to the questions below. Make a list and share that list with someone else.

What behaviors need to change in my life for me to become more like Jesus?

_____

_____

_____

What values need to change in my life for me to become more like Jesus?

_____

_____

_____

Chapter Journal

I will: _____

_____

_____

I will: _____

_____

_____

I will: _____

_____

_____

I will: _____

_____

_____

Notes:

_____

_____

_____

_____

Chapter 2
Trainer's Guide

⬅ Look Back

Give everyone a chance to share, hear from others, and be held accountable. Focus on encouragement, celebration, and following through with assignments.
- Have <u>everyone</u> **report back on how they shared their story and followed through with what they said they would do since the last training.**
- Review the expected outcome and key principle from Chapter 1. Summarize the key points learned from the previous week. Discuss if you have seen any spiritual fruit in your life over the past week.
- Remind everyone that training is for trainers. Are they training others with what they are learning?

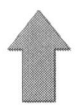

⬆ Look Up

This chapter introduces and explains the importance of ongoing personal growth as a Christlike leader. It is critical that you focus on the following as you train through this chapter:
- Growing from one level of leadership to the next will result in increased challenges and pressure. Commitment to intentional personal growth is required to make progress.
- Growth requires learning new skills, behaviors, and the ability to trust those you are leading with the work of the ministry.
- **Remember to highlight the expected outcome and key principle!** Encourage memorization of key Scripture verses.
- **Hearing from God:** At the end of each chapter, allow for a time of silent prayer and reflection, specifically looking for what each person should do in response to God speaking to their heart.

➡ Look Forward

Before moving on to the assignment for the week, ask the following questions:
- How is God speaking to your heart today?
- How is God calling you to greater obedience?
- What will you do today & this week in response to God's voice?

Assignment for this Chapter:
- Based on the descriptions of the various levels of leadership, use the Personal Development Plan to create a practical plan for personal development and growth.
- **Continue sharing your story and God's story this week. Have you reviewed your list of people you are praying for daily?**
- Write your I will statement(s) in the chapter journal.

Chapter 2
Growing as a Christlike Leader

Expected Outcome: Every disciple maker will intentionally grow as a Christlike leader while they equip others to do the same.

At this point in your training, you have started making disciple makers. Some of you have even been part of planting new churches. In order to support and accelerate this growth, new skills, values, and behaviors will be required. What has worked in the past may not continue to work the same way in the future. This is because different levels of leadership exist. To move from one level to the next requires changes and personal growth.

Growing from one level of leadership to the next will result in increased challenges and pressure. As you grow and progress, you will need to spend more time leading others and developing the values, behaviors, skills, and time allocations required for success. All of this is built on an ever-growing foundation of Christlike character and integrity.

What it takes to grow as a leader:
- <u>Values & Behaviors:</u> what people believe is important and becomes the focus of their efforts and behaviors.
- <u>Skills:</u> new capabilities required for success and a willingness to take higher level assignments.
- <u>Time Allocations:</u> new time frames that determine how work should be done.

TTI has connected all of the key positions to leadership levels. This way, people can grow with a clear understanding of the character, values, knowledge, and skills required to handle particular levels of leadership. Consider the following 3 levels of leadership:

Level 1 - Seed Sower - Individual Contributor

- Motivated by Jesus' command to spread the Gospel and make disciples, they lovingly do so—in spite of fear or obstacles—with simple, childlike faith.
- Able to use simple tools to faithfully share their story and God's story.
- Accountability, ongoing encouragement, and immediate feedback is highly motivating.
- Begin by reaching their friends, family, neighbors, and the people they encounter in their daily life.

Level 2 - Disciple Maker & Church Planter - Leader of Individuals

- Level 1 Seed Sower +
- Gathers new believers into prayer fellowships and discipleship groups/churches.
- Able to lead new believers in prayer, participative (Discovery) Bible study, hearing from God, and effectively model Level 1 skills.
- Able to train and mobilize faithful new believers (using Disciples Making Disciples - Level 1 and Disciples Making Disciples - Level 2), focusing on empowering emerging leaders to greater responsibility.
- Begin taking ownership for personal spiritual growth and intentionally looking to identify spiritual gifts in others.
- Growing understanding of what it takes for a healthy church to function and figure out how to handle the ordinances (Baptism/Communion).

Level 3 - Trainer & Mentor - Leader of Leaders

- Level 2 Disciple Maker & Church Planter +

- Multiplying disciple makers and planting churches that are multiple generations deep.
- Able to effectively cast vision and communicate the philosophy of multiplying disciples and churches in a clear and simple way. They are thinking about 2nd, 3rd, and 4th generation churches.
- Able to train, mentor, and teach Level 2 Leaders through TTI materials in a way that results in disciples making disciples and churches planting churches.
- Display a willingness to empower church planters and release authority.
- Quick and willing to delegate responsibility to others with a method that ensures follow-through.
- Developing a better awareness of what results in the highest return on the investment of time, efforts, and energy.

Expectations for Level 1 - Seed Sowers
- <u>Values:</u> Love God and love people. Faithful obedience to Scripture.
- <u>Skills:</u> Able to use simple tools (Sharing My Story & God's Story) and model for others.
- <u>Time Allocation:</u> Some extra time is spent prayer walking, but majority of effort is simply being more intentional with people they know and normally encounter.

Growing from Level 1 to Level 2

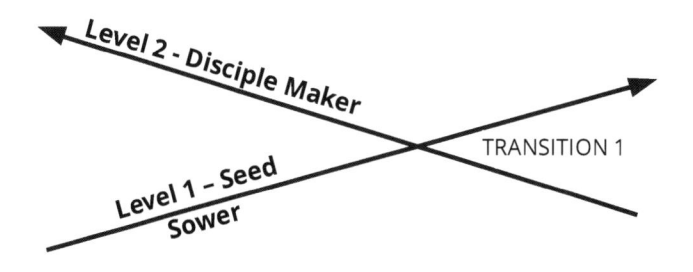

Requirements to Move to Level 2 - Disciple Maker/Church Planter
- <u>Values:</u> Relationship and time with God and others becomes more important and consistent. Investing in people takes higher levels of priority than before.
- <u>Skills:</u> Increasingly confident in communicating biblical truths as a result of discipleship training. Effective in modeling Level 1 skills and careful to practice what is preached.
- <u>Time Allocation:</u> More time is spent in training, planning, fellowship, and discipling believers to become disciple makers.

Practical Notes for Moving from Level 1 to Level 2

The primary focus at this leadership transition is to get to a point where you can effectively lead more than just yourself. **The ability to lead others is a basic requirement for Level 2 - Disciple Makers/Church Planters.** Remember: every believer is called to be a disciple maker. Just as you have made disciples, it is now time to help others do the same. The expectations you have on those you are attempting to lead will greatly impact what they do, what they value, and even how they approach the Christian life.

At Level 2, you now need to begin focusing more on accomplishing tasks through the efforts of others. You must no longer focus only on your own efforts but the efforts of those you are training and discipling. This may result in a temporary decrease in effectiveness because you are no longer the only one involved in making things happen. **This is normal and to be expected!** You will make mistakes and sometimes you may feel less effective or uncomfortable when this happens. **Resist the temptation to take control and try to do everything on your own.** A new Leadership Level requires skills, behaviors, and the ability to trust those you are leading with the work of the ministry.

Group Discussion - Read and discuss the following story as it relates to moving from Level 1 to Level 2.

As Samuel goes through the Disciples Making Disciples - Level 1 training, he is an active Seed Sower. He personally decides when he will share the Gospel and how much time he will spend in prayer, devotions, and talking to people. Everything he does is connected back to his own individual contribution (even though his trainer helps and encourages). So far, Samuel has reached three new families and started meeting regularly for prayer and fellowship.

As Samuel begins to disciple these new believers, he realizes that some take things very seriously (as he did), while others seem to resist or do not show as much interest. It is clear he no longer has direct control of the situation. If Samuel continues to do everything on his own, he will be limited in the ability to grow the fellowship into a church or develop these believers into disciple makers. He is beginning to realize if everything depends on his own efforts, the work will likely collapse as soon as he leaves. With this in mind, Samuel focuses more time investing in the faithful and fruitful new believers and challenges them with intentional discipleship.

Group Discussion: How can Samuel continue to grow through the first transition and move to Level 2?

Developmental Assignment: 1st Leadership Transition

As you go through this book, you are likely somewhere between Level 1 and Level 2. Understanding the first two levels and what it will take to successfully move to the next level (if you have not already) is very relevant. As you attempt

to grow personally (while you train others also), keep in mind that you and those you are training probably fit one of the below descriptions:
- **Unable or uninterested to move from Level 1 to Level 2.**
  These people are likely inconsistent, not self-motivated, and may not display spiritual fruit.
- **Currently going through or stuck in the transition from Level 1 to Level 2.**
  These people are faithful and committed but are still struggling with the transition from doing things themselves to leading others and influencing them.
- **Successfully made it through the transition and are now at Level 2.**
  These people often do more than assigned or expected. They are self-motivated, consistent, offer creative ideas for improvement, and have already identified who they can disciple.

Use the development plan template (at the end of this chapter) to help create a Personal Development Plan that identifies where you are, where you desire to be, and how you will get there. Be sure to be clear on expectations and reasonable timelines so you can be held accountable. Remember, one of the keys to growing is identifying practical assignments that will test your abilities and challenge your thinking.

2nd Leadership Transition: Level 2 to Level 3
For those who are already at Level 2, we would encourage you to consider how you can progress to Level 3.

Expectations at Level 2 - Disciple Makers/Church Planters:
- <u>Values:</u> Spending time and growing in relationship with God and others is important and consistent. Caring about the development of others has become a regular part of life.
- <u>Skills:</u> Increasingly confident and competent when training others through simple discipleship materials.

Becoming clearer when communicating biblical truths. Effective in modeling Level 1 skills and careful to practice what is preached.
- Time Allocation: More time is spent training, planning, in fellowship, and discipling believers to become disciple makers. There is also greater awareness of time management and planning ahead.

Growing from Level 2 to Level 3

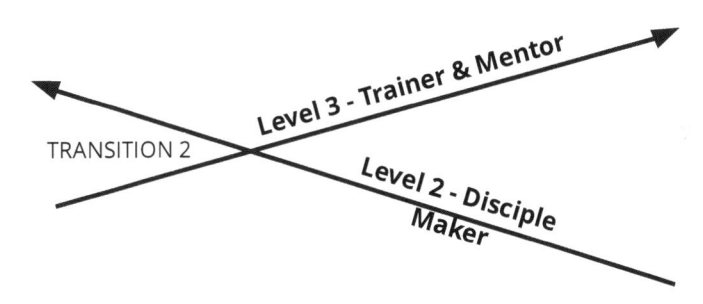

```
TRANSITION 2    Level 3 - Trainer & Mentor
                Level 2 - Disciple Maker
```

Requirements to move to Level 3 - Trainer & Mentor
- Values: Internal ownership of TTI's core values, mission, philosophy, and commitment to reproducing disciple makers and church planters. Mentoring, developing, and empowering others becomes increasingly important. Primary focus on the empowerment of others, with the goal of spiritual fruit, church health, and multiple generations.
- Skills: Effectively cast vision and communicate the philosophy of multiplying disciples and churches in a clear and simple way. Train, mentor, and teach Level 2 Leaders through TTI curriculum in a way that results in disciples making disciples and churches planting churches. Quick to delegate tasks and responsibility, solve problems, follow up, hold others accountable, and form leadership teams. Deal with conflict and disputes between others. Strategic planning, budgeting, and coordinating activities.
- Time Allocation: More time is spent training faithful and fruitful Level 2 Leaders. Additional time is given to

ongoing personal development and receiving coaching from Level 3 & 4 Leaders.

Practical Notes for Moving from Level 2 to Level 3

The primary focus as you go through this leadership transition is **learning to balance the leadership of people with the growing responsibilities of ministry.** It is important to learn how to delegate responsibility in a way that ensures accountability for what has been delegated.

Developing people and building strong teams requires a process of **giving direction, ensuring alignment, and seeing commitment in others.** This means your role is increasingly focused on ensuring there is a clear sense of direction (where to go), alignment (what to do as you go), and commitment (perseverance as you go).

The need for personal integrity and character has never been more important. Level 3 Leaders have the greatest impact and influence on whether or not TTI is producing disciple makers and church planters. When we lack strong character and competency, our influence will not be nearly as effective. This will likely lead to a lack of growth in our lives and the lives of those we are leading. If you are seeing a decreased rate of growth or no growth at all, there may be an area of weakness in your character or competency. This is why ongoing personal development, accountability, training, and mentoring are essential for growth, especially while you are training others!

It is important to avoid extra biblical qualifications as you lead disciple makers to plant churches. Do your best to avoid unnecessary traditions and cultural requirements for church leadership that do not fit the priorities of Scripture *(1 Timothy 3:1-7; Titus 1:6-9)* or the principles of multiplication *(2 Timothy 2:2).*
Keep your view of the church as practical as possible. To see a

growing movement of disciples and church planters, you must keep things simple and deal with conflict as it happens. Make sure those you lead have a clear focus on the King and His Kingdom as their first core value.

Group Discussion: Read and discuss the following story as it relates to moving from Level 2 to Level 3.

Thomas has been in TTI training for nearly 1 year. He has done a great job of consistently sharing his faith and training others to do the same. God has blessed these efforts, and Thomas has been able to plant a growing church with ten families in his home. They are nearly out of space and don't know what to do next.

Thomas has also identified two Tituses and together they are praying and planning how they will plant a second-generation church in a neighboring village. While Thomas is part of a TTI Training Center, he is also taking his Tituses through Disciples Making Disciples - Levels 1 and 2 to aid in their discipleship. He will need more oversight from his Paul, serious mentoring, encouragement, and practical experience to be able to get to the second generation of church planting.

Group Discussion: How can Thomas move through the second transition and move to Level 3?

Developmental Assignment: 2nd Leadership Transition
As mentioned previously, you are likely between Levels 1 and 2, but some of you will be between Levels 2 and 3. As you attempt to grow personally (while training others also), keep in mind the following descriptions for most people between Levels 2 and 3.
- **Unable or uninterested in moving from Level 2 to Level 3.**
  These people have been able to lead a few to Christ but have not invested the time and energy to move them

to greater maturity in discipleship. They struggle to communicate biblical truths and may not take their own personal development or growth very seriously.
- **Currently going through or stuck in the transition from Level 2 to Level 3.**
  These people have formed a small church of new believers and are experiencing mixed results when it comes to developing and mobilizing them into disciple makers. They have the character but may lack or need to improve the skills required to move to Level 3.
- **Successfully made it through the transition and are now at Level 3.**
  These people show a desire to build lasting relationships and are actively mobilizing disciple makers. They are already thinking about 2nd and 3rd generation disciples and churches. They are not only able to do Level 2 work but can also operate at the level of the Paul.

Assignment for this Chapter: Based on the descriptions of the various levels of leadership in this chapter, use the Personal Development Plan on the next page to create a practical plan for personal development and growth.

Continue sharing your story and God's story with those on your list. Share your successes and difficulties with those being trained.

Personal Development Plan

Name: _____ Date: _____

```
TRANSITION 2
Level 3 - Trainer & Mentor
Level 2 - Disciple Maker
Level 1 - Seed Sower
TRANSITION 1
```

Using the chart above, mark what you think is your current level of leadership and the level you desire to be.

What will it take to get to the next level? Review the descriptions of the leadership levels and the one you are targeting. Be clear with expectations, and keep your personal developmental assignments practical, measurable, and focused on developing the right values, skills, and behaviors required at the next level.

Values to change: _____
_____

Skills to develop: _____
_____

Sit with your trainer and come up with a plan that will help you move to the next level of leadership.

_____
_____
_____

When you will review your progress: _____

*Is there anyone who comes to mind that you can help create their own Personal Development Plan? How can you help them?

Chapter Journal

I will: _____

_____

_____

I will: _____

_____

_____

I will: _____

_____

_____

I will: _____

_____

_____

Notes:

_____

_____

_____

_____

Chapter 3
Trainer's Guide

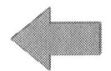

⬅ Look Back

Give everyone a chance to share, hear from others, and be held accountable. Focus on encouragement, celebration, and following through with assignments.

- **Have <u>everyone</u> report back on how they shared their story and followed through with what they said they would do since the last training.**
- Review the expected outcome and three levels of leadership introduced in Chapter 2.
- Did you create your personal development plan? How is it going?
- Remind everyone that training is for trainers. Are they training others with what they are learning?

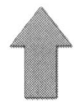

⬆ Look Up

This chapter introduces and explains the importance of the Bible. It is critical that you focus on the following as you train through this chapter:

- The Bible is trustworthy, complete, and for your benefit.
- Correctly interpreting Scripture is essential for correctly applying Scripture in your life.
- Scripture helps us understand and apply other Scripture. The more you read or listen, the more you will learn and understand and accordingly be able to apply and train others.
- **Remember to highlight the expected outcome and key principle!** Encourage memorization of key Scripture verses.
- **Hearing from God:** At the end of each chapter, allow for a time of silent prayer and reflection, specifically looking for what each person should do in response to God speaking to their heart.

Group Activity: Ask each person in the group to talk about someone they deeply respect and trust. Discuss why you are more likely to believe in someone you trust.

Model & Practice: Every trainer should emphasize the importance of reading God's Word frequently and consistently. Explain how you read and study the Bible. What day and time? How much do you read? What do you do before and after you read? Show how knowledge can be turned into practice by focusing on the practical teachings in the Scriptures.

➡ Look Forward

Before moving on to the assignment for the week, ask the following questions:
- How is God speaking to your heart today?
- How is God calling you to greater obedience?
- What will you do today & this week in response to God's voice?

Assignment for this Chapter:
- Spend extra time in prayer this week asking God to place a desire in your heart for His Word. The ability to read or listen to God's Word is a privilege that not everyone has!
- **Continue sharing your story and God's story this week. Have you reviewed your list of people you are daily praying for?**
- Write your I will statement(s) in the chapter journal.

Chapter 3
Introduction to the Bible

Expected Outcome: Every disciple maker will see how God's Word is trustworthy and learn to interpret it accurately.

Imagine finding a letter that was written 100 years ago. You do not know who wrote it or why. You do not know the person to whom the letter is written. You do not know the people, places, or even some of the words that it mentions. Now imagine you were asked to explain the letter to another person. You might be able to figure out some things, but you might make some wrong assumptions as well.

In order to explain the letter correctly, you would need to know more about the authors, original recipients, and the purpose of the letter. It would also be helpful to know the background of the author and the original recipients.

The same is true of the Bible. If we do not understand where the Bible comes from, how it was written, and why, we may make mistakes when trying to discover and communicate the Bible.

1. ***What is the Bible?*** The Bible is God's written Word. It carries the very breath and character of God. It is through these Holy Scriptures that God communicates with us.

2. ***How did we get the Bible?*** God revealed Himself to people and told them to write down His words completely and accurately, free from error.

3. ***Who wrote the Bible?*** God chose more than 40 people to communicate His message both orally and in writing. These stories and writings were completely inspired by God, historically written, copied, reproduced, and shared with others. These writings form what we call the Bible.

The Bible is an unchanging set of historical events, teachings, and principles. There is nothing to add to or subtract from the Bible; it is complete.

Group Activity: Ask each person in the group to talk about someone they deeply respect and trust. Discuss why you are more likely to believe in someone you trust.

How do we know the Bible is complete?

The Bible says in *Revelation 22:18-19, "I warn everyone who hears the words of the prophecy of this book: if anyone adds to them, God will add to him the plagues described in this book, and if anyone takes away from the words of the book of this prophecy, God will take away his share in the tree of life and in the holy city, which are described in this book."*

These verses refute any attempt to add or subtract from God's Word and remind us as readers to take the Bible seriously.

God gave mankind His Word, along with the responsibility of protecting it, copying it, and translating it. These words were carefully written down and reproduced by individuals who copied the writings by hand. They did this accurately, and the Bible we have today is a result of those copies *(Luke 1:1-4)*. This shows why the Bible is worthy to be trusted as a guide of our faith. It gives all people the opportunity to hear and read God's Word, regardless of their language. **The Bible is the first and most translated book ever!** (You can find the Bible in thousands of languages in written and audio for free at www.bible.is).

To whom was the Bible written?

The Bible was written to all mankind. God reveals Himself to us through His Spirit and His Word. **The Bible is God's Word!**

What is the purpose of the Bible?

The purpose and goal of God's Word is that all may know Him, enter into relationship with Him, worship Him, and make Him known.

Discovering and understanding the Bible is extremely important because nearly everything we know about God comes from it. If you misinterpret or misunderstand it, you can mislead yourself as well as others.

Group Discussion: Consider how your culture is different from the cultures in which the Bible was written. How can you communicate the Bible clearly in your local context?

Key Principle: One of the primary roles of a disciple who makes disciples is to give proper attention to both the meaning of Scripture and its application in their culture.

Some Basics of Interpreting the Bible

Scripture interprets Scripture. If you are unclear on one verse or one chapter, look for other verses and chapters on the same subject to compare and contrast. For example, *Luke 8:5* is interpreted by *Luke 8:11-12.*

"A sower went out to sow his seed. And as he sowed, some fell by the wayside; and it was trampled down, and the birds of the air devoured it" (Luke 8:5).

"Now the parable is this: The seed is the word of God. Those by the wayside are the ones who hear; then the devil comes and takes away the word out of their hearts, lest they should believe and be saved" (Luke 8:11-12).

You can see how *Luke 8:11-12* explains *Luke 8:5*. By knowing and reading Scripture, we can better understand and interpret the different parts of the Bible. **Remember: knowing and understanding must always be connected back to applying, obeying, and training the next generation!**

- Using the Discovery Bible Study method will guide towards correct interpretation and deeper understanding of specific Bible passages. (See next chapter.)
- As a result of carefully applying what we learn in the Bible, we develop right beliefs (called doctrine), which point towards right living.
- **Right Belief** is built on the foundation of proper discovery and understanding of the Bible.
- **Right Living** is built on top of **Right Belief**. What we know from the Bible should impact what we do *(Ephesians 4:17-24)!*

Consider this relationship another way: imagine the process of interpreting the Bible as a house. Discovering and Understanding the Bible would be the foundation; Right Belief would be the walls and structure that rests upon proper discovery. Right Living would be the roof that rests upon Right Belief. Use the drawing on the following page to better understand and explain this principle to others.

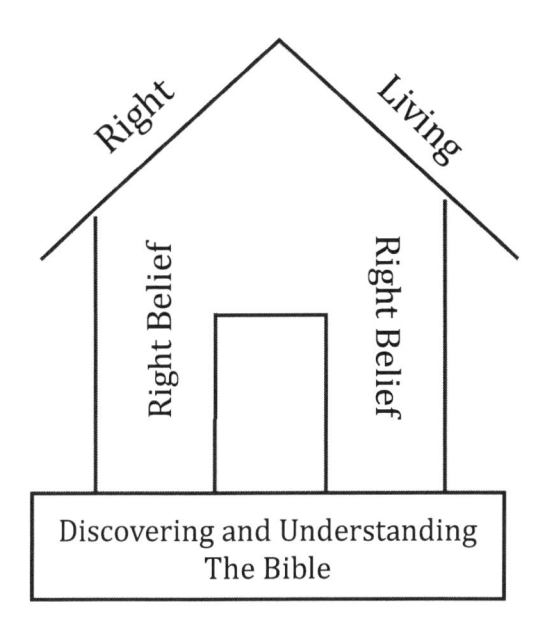

(Diagram: A house shape. Roof labeled "Right" and "Living". Two walls each labeled "Right Belief". Foundation labeled "Discovering and Understanding The Bible".)

Key Principle: Right living comes from right beliefs, and right belief comes from proper discovery and understanding.

Why is it important to learn how to interpret the Bible?

Consider the following story: *One day there was an Ethiopian returning home from a religious pilgrimage. He read from the book of Isaiah in the Bible but was unable to understand what he was reading. God sent a man named Philip to interpret and explain what he was reading. Philip asked him, "Do you understand what you are reading?" The Ethiopian said, "How can I, unless someone guides me?" Philip then gave a proper interpretation of the passage. As a result, the Ethiopian put his faith in Christ. (For the full story, see Acts 8 and Isaiah 53.)*

What is the Bible?

The Bible is God's Word, written down. It is the way that He communicates with us.

How did we get the Bible?

__Inspiration__: The words in the Bible are God-breathed ... they are completely accurate and free from error.

How was the Bible written (transmitted)?

The Bible was communicated orally ... and historically written down and reproduced.

How did we get the Bible in my language?

The Original Languages (Hebrew, Greek & Aramaic) were translated into local languages/dialects.

Model & Practice: The Importance of Personal Bible Study

Every trainer should show how you read and study the Bible. What day and time? How much do you read? What do you do before and after you read? How do you put what you hear from God into practice? How do you share with others what you learn and do?

Group Discussion: How does understanding the way the Bible was made impact your faith? It does little good to know the truths of Scripture yet fail to put them into practice. With whom can you share what you have learned from this chapter?

Assignment for this Chapter: Spend extra time in prayer this week asking God to place a desire in your heart for His Word. The ability to read or listen to God's Word is a privilege that not everyone has!

Continue sharing your story and God's story this week. Have you reviewed your list of people you are daily praying for?

Chapter Journal

I will: _____

_____

_____

I will: _____

_____

_____

I will: _____

_____

_____

I will: _____

_____

_____

Notes:

_____

_____

_____

_____

Chapters 4-6
Trainer's Guide

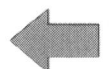

⬅ Look Back

Give everyone a chance to share, hear from others, and be held accountable. Focus on encouragement, celebration, and following through with assignments.

- **Have <u>everyone</u> report back on how they shared their story and followed through with what they said they would do since the last training.**
- Review the expected outcome from Chapter 3.
- Did you lead a Discovery Bible Study? How did it go?

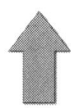

⬆ Look Up

Chapters 4-6 focus on communicating God's Word in different sized groups: small, medium, and large. It is critical that you focus on the following as you train through this chapter:

- Different sized groups require different strategies, models, and lessons. No group will be identical to another group.
- The goal of any size group is to make maturing disciples who make disciples. Churches are training grounds for future church planters and disciple makers.
- As your group grows, invest more training and time with the people you believe have the potential to be leaders of the next generation of disciple makers.
- **Remember to highlight the expected outcome and key principle from each chapter!**
- **Hearing from God:** At the end of each chapter, allow for a time of silent prayer and reflection, specifically looking for what each person should do in response to God speaking to their heart.

Group Activity: How are you intentionally praying for the people you are leading? A large part of being a disciple maker and church planter is caring for those you are shepherding. Discuss how you can make improvements and come up with some practical steps. Most importantly, put them into practice.

Model & Practice: Model how you would lead each size group, so it is clear exactly how things should look.

⇒ Look Forward

Before moving on to the assignment for the week, ask the following questions:
- How is God speaking to your heart today?
- How is God calling you to greater obedience?
- What will you do today & this week in response to God's voice?

Assignments for these Chapters:
- Review the suggestions of what to do when you gather together based on the actual size group you are leading. Put the suggested steps into practice as you gather with those you are leading. After a few weeks, review with your trainer what seems to be working well and any areas you are finding difficult.
- **Continue sharing your story and God's Story.**
- **Write I will statement(s) in your chapter journal.**

Chapter 4
Communicating God's Word in Small Groups

Expected Outcome: Every disciple maker will lead Group Discovery Bible Studies and practice communicating the Bible in their group.

As new churches are being planted, it is important to be clear on the role each person has in the church. (See DMD - Level 1, Chapter 10.) The ultimate aim is to move disciples and churches towards maturity and multiplication. Churches often begin as a result of new believers gathering together on a daily or regular basis for prayer, fellowship, encouragement, and Bible study. This happens in different locations, styles, and group sizes. TTI's hope is that every church planter will be intentional and purposeful as they begin gathering disciples together. **Regardless of the size of the group, it is important for every disciple (new or old) to regularly hear from God and faithfully respond in obedience.**

Key Principle: No matter the size of the group you start, the focus and priority should always be on multiplication and reproduction.

As you begin to gather disciples together regularly, you will need to learn how to communicate God's Word in different size groups. The next three chapters introduce three different group sizes and explain what TTI suggests is the best approach for each.
- Smaller groups consisting of 3-15 people
- Medium groups consisting of 16-50 people
- Larger groups consisting of 50+ people

There are similarities and differences among each of the three group sizes. For example, the role of the leaders will change depending upon the size of the group. As the group grows in size, so do the costs and the space required for meeting together. The amount of time you have when you gather and even what you do when you are together is directly connected to the size, space, and dynamics of the group. What works well in smaller groups may not work well in medium or larger groups. Carefully consider the similarities and differences so you can lead your group well!

Model & Practice: Leading Your Group Well

Model how you would lead a small, medium, and large group, so it is clear exactly how things should look.

All suggestions are given as a guide to follow what TTI feels is the best way to lead towards reproduction and multiplication of disciples and churches. Every partner has the freedom and flexibility to apply what they feel is the most appropriate method in their local context.

Smaller Groups
3-15 People

General observations from groups of this size:
- **Examples:** Micro-church, house fellowship, DBS group.
- **Locations they meet:** Houses, businesses, parks, coffee shops, salons, community center, any possible space to meet regularly.
- **Cost:** Normally, there is no financial cost or rent associated with meeting in this size group.
- **Level of formality:** Non-formal.
- **Sitting style:** In a circle facing one another in chairs or at a table.

Role of the leader: Leading the church and modeling for next generation disciples.
- The church planter of this group serves as the main leader, teacher, shepherd, and disciple maker.

Role of key next generation leaders: Learning and assisting.
- These emerging leaders are disciple makers who assist the leader and actively participate in the church.

Suggestions for what to do when you gather:
This gathering size is very relational, and it is easy for all the believers to know one another. It is easy for each person to be heard and be held accountable. It is recommended to follow a Group Discovery Bible Study approach as introduced in the previous chapter.

Assignment for the Chapter: Do a Group Discovery Bible Study this week.

Continue sharing your story and God's story with 1 person from your prayer list every day. **Be sure to report back to your trainer what happens!**

Model for Smaller Groups:

⬅ Look Back

- Welcome any new people and thank them for joining.
- Give everyone a chance to share how God is at work in and through their lives, hear from one another, and be held accountable. **Focus on encouragement, celebration, and following through with commitments.**
- Summarize the key points learned from the previous gathering and tell how you applied them to your life and shared them with others.

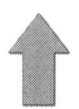

⬆ Look Up

- Spend intentional time in worship, prayer, and fellowship (singing, dancing, eating together, etc.).
- Do a Group Discovery Bible Study. Encourage everyone's participation (even new people and children).
- Observe the ordinances from time to time (Baptism & Communion).
- Give an opportunity for sacrificial giving.

➡ Look Forward

- Before you Look Forward, pause for a moment in prayer and ask some of the following questions:
  - How is God speaking to your heart today?
  - How is God calling you to greater obedience?
  - What will you do today & this week in response to God's voice?
- Based on what was learned from God's Word, how everyone is hearing God's voice, identify action steps for the week:
  - Encourage each person to share what they plan to do (I will …)
  - Encourage everyone to share the love of Christ with the lost world.
  - Identify ways you can meet the needs of the people in the group as well as outside the group.

Chapter Journal

I will: _____

_____

_____

I will: _____

_____

_____

I will: _____

_____

_____

I will: _____

_____

_____

Notes:

_____

_____

_____

_____

Chapter 5
Communicating God's Word in Medium Groups

Expected Outcome: Every disciple maker will lead Group Discovery Bible Studies and practice communicating the Bible in their group.

Moving from Smaller Groups to Medium Groups

As a young church grows bigger, the ability to sit together and hear from one another becomes increasingly challenging. Hearing from each person and providing an opportunity to share and be held accountable is critical. With this in mind, it is encouraged to consider starting new smaller-sized groups before growing existing groups to a medium size. This way each person has the time and attention to share and be held accountable.

Remember, **everyone can hear from God directly.** If your growing church does grow beyond 15 people, consider breaking up into 2-3 groups when Looking Back and Looking Forward (For example: one group for men, one for women, and another for youth/children). Be careful to avoid the trap of some people coming and going without ever being held accountable. **Holding one another accountable is one of the most loving things we can do for one another.** This should be done out of a genuine desire for others to know the Lord more deeply and experience the joy and fulfillment of living life abundantly, being conformed to the image of Christ *(Ephesians 4:13).*

For those leading a growing church, it will be important to look for the faithful and available disciples who are willing and able to take on more responsibilities with follow-up and discipling efforts. **Invest most heavily in those who are faithful in applying and passing on what they learn to others.** (To learn more about this, it is recommended that you consider getting higher level intentional training from a trainer mentor.)

With a growing church, it is important that the leadership team has a plan to plant a next generation church in a new place or identify a larger place to meet before the current place of worship becomes full. As you expand, focus on places where there are no churches and people groups missed or ignored by the existing churches.

Medium Groups
16-50 People

General observations from groups of this size:
- **Examples:** Micro-church, house church, fellowship, etc.
- **Locations they meet:** Houses, businesses, community center, parks, unused church buildings, any possible space to meet regularly.
- **Cost:** None or minimal financial cost associated with meeting in this group size.
- **Level of formality:** Non-formal, semi-formal, or formal.
- **Sitting style:** In a circle facing one another, in chairs, or at tables.

Role of the leader: Leading the church and modeling for next generation disciples.
- The leader of this group serves as the main teacher, shepherd, and disciple maker. Faithful disciples should be given intentional opportunities to help lead the group (leading the Discovery Bible Study, prayer/worship, etc.).

Role of key next generation leaders: Learning and assisting.
- Faithful disciples are given more opportunities to serve in the church in a variety of roles like training, teaching, serving communion, leading the group, etc. They will begin to be challenged to consider what it would take to start new groups.

Suggestions for what to do when you gather:
This gathering size is still very relational, and the believers

generally all know one another. However, without being very intentional, it will become increasingly more difficult for each person to be heard and held accountable. As the group grows, it will be critical to intentionally develop leaders and plan for the next steps. It is recommended to follow a Group Discovery Bible Study approach as taught in this book by dividing into smaller groups led by faithful disciples.

It is important that the leadership team has a plan to plant a next generation church in a new place or identify a larger place to meet before the current place of worship becomes full. As you expand, focus on places where there are no churches and people groups are missed or ignored by the existing churches.

Group Discussion: How are you intentionally praying for the people you are leading? A large part of being a disciple maker and church planter is caring for those you are leading. Discuss how you can you do a better job and come up with some practical steps. Most importantly, put them into practice.

Assignment for this Chapter: Continue leading Group Discovery Bible Studies as your group grows.

Continue sharing your story and God's story with 1 person from your prayer list every day. **Be sure to report back to your trainer what happens!**

Model for Medium Groups:

⬅ Look Back

- Welcome any new people and thank them for joining.
- Break up into smaller groups in order to give everyone a chance to share how God is at work in and through their lives, hear from one another, and be held accountable. **Focus on encouragement, celebration, and following through with commitments.**
- Summarize the key points learned from the previous gathering and tell how you applied them to your life and shared them with others.

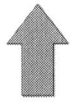

⬆ Look Up

- Come back together as a larger group and spend intentional time in worship, prayer, and fellowship (singing, dancing, eating together, etc.).
- Observe the ordinances from often.
- Give an opportunity for sacrificial giving.
- Divide back into smaller groups and do a Group Discovery Bible Study. Encourage everyone's participation (even new people and children).

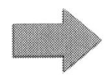

➡ Look Forward

- Before looking forward, pause for a moment in prayer and ask some of the following questions:
  o How is God speaking to your heart today?
  o How is God calling you to greater obedience?
  o What will you do today & this week in response to God's voice?
- Break up into smaller groups and based on what was learned from the Bible study and how everyone is hearing God's voice, identify action steps for the week:
  o Encourage everyone to share what they will do - "I will"
  o Encourage everyone to share the love of Christ with the lost.
  o Identify ways you can meet the needs of the people in the church as well as outside the church.

Chapter Journal

I will: _____

_____

_____

I will: _____

_____

_____

I will: _____

_____

_____

I will: _____

_____

_____

Notes:

_____

_____

_____

_____

_____

Chapter 6
Communicating God's Word in Large Groups

Expected Outcome: Every disciple maker will lead Group Discovery Bible Studies and practice communicating the Bible in their group.

Moving from Medium Groups to Larger Groups

If a church grows beyond 50 people, the dynamics of the group will quickly change. **Resist the tendency to shift focus inward on the people already in your group and continue to look outward to reach new disciples.**

There will likely be more formality and clearer expectations on:
- When people should arrive.
- When to start the group discussion.
- Who is supposed to do what.

All of these details should be planned clearly. It is possible that the believers in the church will be able to support the church planter financially and perhaps will even be able to donate or purchase land, construct a more permanent meeting space, etc. Keep in mind there are positive and negative effects associated with any decision like this. All decisions should be done according to the local context and resources. **Remember: The Church is not a building ... it is the body of Christ.** (TTI does not financially contribute towards buildings but invests in leaders and disciple makers.)

Larger Groups
50+ People

General observations from groups of this size:
- **Examples:** Church, fellowship.
- **Locations they meet:** In an open space, under sheds, in a community center, in a building, in a business, or in any possible space to meet regularly.
- **Cost:** Minimal or significant financial cost.
- **Level of formality:** Semi-formal or formal.
- **Sitting style:** In rows, on chairs, on the floor, or on mats.

Role of the leader: Leading the church and modeling for next generation disciples.
- The leader of this group serves as the primary equipper of the next generation of leaders. The focus should be on spiritual maturity and healthy multiplication.

Role of key next generation leaders: Learning and assisting.
- Faithful disciples can lead in a variety of ways and roles. They are equipped and empowered to start their own group with next generation disciples.

In TTI's model of training, the faithful few discipled by Timothys are called Tituses. As more churches are planted, the Titus has the opportunity to naturally progress to the level of Timothy; Timothy to the level of Paul; Paul to the level of Master Trainer; Master Trainer to the level of Movement Leader.

Suggestions for what to do when you gather:
Without being very intentional, it will be impossible for each person to be heard and held accountable. As the group grows, you must be very careful to plan for the next steps. The leadership team should have a plan to plant multiple generations of churches in areas with unreached people

groups and in areas where there are no churches.

With a larger group, it may be more natural to begin teaching or preaching directly from the Word of God. As you grow and become comfortable with this, it can be a good method of communicating God's Word.

Remember: As you gather together in a larger group, do not lose emphasis on disciple making, multiplying new groups, and accountability to apply what one has learned and pass it on to the next generation.

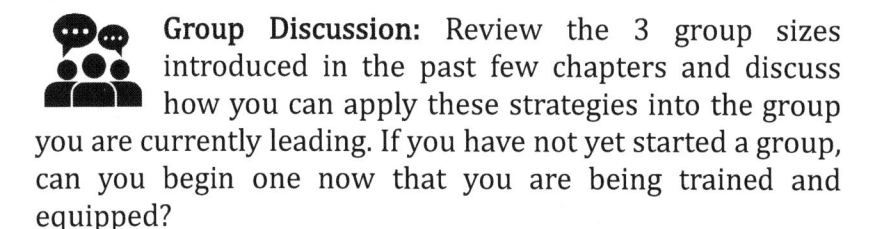

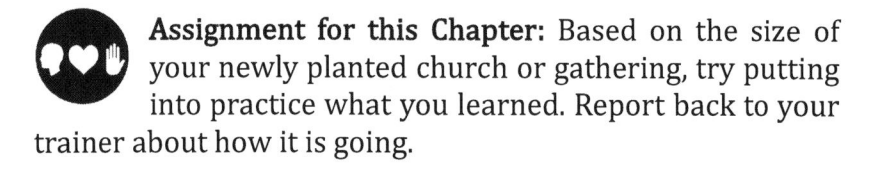

Group Discussion: Review the 3 group sizes introduced in the past few chapters and discuss how you can apply these strategies into the group you are currently leading. If you have not yet started a group, can you begin one now that you are being trained and equipped?

Assignment for this Chapter: Based on the size of your newly planted church or gathering, try putting into practice what you learned. Report back to your trainer about how it is going.

Continue sharing your story and God's story with 1 person from your prayer list every day. **Be sure to report back to your trainer what happens!**

Model for Larger Groups:

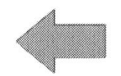

⬅ Look Back

- Welcome any new people and thank them for joining.
- Either break into smaller groups or consider having groups meet during the week so that everyone has a chance to share how God is at work in and through their lives, hear from one another, and be held accountable. **Focus on encouragement, celebration, and following through with commitments.** <u>If you do not keep the same expectations on accountability, people will likely drift away from taking personal responsibility to be a disciple maker. Make sure this does not happen!</u>
- Encourage a few people to share testimonies of how God is at work and how they are applying what they are learning. Remind everyone that the expectation is both to apply and to share with others.

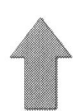

⬆ Look Up

- Spend intentional time in worship, prayer, fellowship, and communicating God's Word by teaching or preaching (singing, dancing, eating together, etc.).
- Observe the ordinances from time to time (Baptism & Communion).
- Give an opportunity for sacrificial giving.

➡ Look Forward

- Pause for a moment in prayer and ask some of the following questions:
   - How is God speaking to your heart today?
   - How is God calling you to greater obedience?

- - What will you do today & this week in response to God's voice?
- Reinforce that everyone has the ability to hear God's voice and encourage everyone to identify action steps for the week:
  - Encourage each person to share what they plan to do in their smaller groups. (I will ...)
  - Encourage everyone to share the love of Christ with the lost world.
  - Identify ways you can meet the needs of the people in the church as well as outside the church.

Chapter Journal

I will: _____

_____

_____

I will: _____

_____

_____

I will: _____

_____

_____

I will: _____

_____

_____

Notes:

_____

_____

_____

_____

_____

Chapters 7-8
Trainer's Guide

⬅ Look Back

Give everyone a chance to share, hear from one another, and be held accountable. Focus on encouragement, appreciation, celebration, and following through with assignments.
- **Have <u>everyone</u> report back on how they shared their story and God's story and followed through with what they said they would do since the last training.**
- Discuss how you have put into practice the things learned from Chapters 4-6 on leading different sized groups. How is it going?
- What is working well? In what areas are you still not clear? Spend some time celebrating the victories you are experiencing and also praying for those who are struggling.

⬆ Look Up

Chapters 7-8 focus on the story of the Bible, beginning in the Old Testament. It is essential that you focus on the following as you train through this chapter:
- The Old Testament contains different types of literature. Knowing these types is important for correctly reading and interpreting the Old Testament.
- The nation of Israel was in a continual cycle of faithfulness and then unfaithfulness to God. As you read or listen to the Old Testament, take note of the way God responds to those who remain faithful.
- The Old Testament is relevant and important for both new and mature believers.
- **Remember to highlight the expected outcome and key principle!** Encourage memorization of key Scripture verses.
- **Hearing from God:** At the end of each chapter, allow for a time of silent prayer and reflection, specifically looking for what each person should do in response to God speaking to their heart.

Group Activity: Discuss your favorite book or part of the Old Testament. If you have not started to read or listen to the Old Testament yet, begin with Genesis.

Model & Practice: Every trainer should be leading Discovery Bible Studies from different parts of the Old Testament. Being able to communicate the stories and principles of the Old Testament is essential for every disciple maker and church planter.

Look Forward

Before moving on to the assignment for the week, ask the following questions:
- How is God speaking to your heart today?
- How is God calling you to greater obedience?
- What will you do today & this week in response to God's voice?

Assignment for these Chapters:
- Listening or reading through each book of the Old Testament in its entirety will greatly help you understand the full story of the Bible. Begin using the Old Testament Reading Guide located in the back of this book to keep track of your progress while reading the whole Old Testament.
- Continue sharing your story and God's story with 1 person from your prayer list every day. **Be sure to report back to your trainer what happens.**
- Write your I will statement(s) in the chapter journal.

Chapter 7
The Story of the Bible
God's Word to Humanity

Expected Outcome: As every disciple maker learns the story of the Bible, they will know the heart of God and be encouraged to faithfully follow His instruction.

Introduction to the Old Testament

Key Verse: *2 Timothy 3:16-17 – "All Scripture is given by inspiration of God, and is profitable for doctrine, for reproof, for correction, for instruction in righteousness, that the man of God may be complete, thoroughly equipped for every good work."*

The Bible is made up of two parts: The Old and New Testaments. The Old Testament contains 39 books and the New Testament contains 27. The Old Testament was written by God through kings, shepherds, warriors, prophets, and many others over a period of more than 1,000 years. The Old Testament:
- Begins with the creation of the world and the origins of all mankind and covers human history all the way to 400 years before the birth of Jesus.
- Tells the story of God and the family He chose to be His people: the Israelites (also called the people of Israel or Jews).
- Reveals God's mighty power and His desire for His people to follow Him faithfully.

Group Discussion: Discuss your favorite book or part of the Old Testament. If you have not started to read or listen to the Old Testament yet, begin with Genesis.

The books of the Old Testament are sometimes divided into four sections:

- **The Law:** Contains the earliest history of the Jewish people and God's instructions for their lives.
- **The History:** The record of ancient Israel's rise and decline as a kingdom and nation.
- **Poetry & Wisdom:** Contains songs of worship, collections of wise sayings, and instructions for how one should live.
- **The Prophets:** Records God's message through the men He chose to reveal His blessings, judgments, and promises.

Below, the books of the Old Testament are divided into these four categories:

The Law	History	Poetry & Wisdom	Prophets
Genesis	Joshua	Job	Isaiah
Exodus	Judges	Psalms	Jeremiah
Leviticus	Ruth	Proverbs	Lamentations
Numbers	1 Samuel	Ecclesiastes	Ezekiel
Deuteronomy	2 Samuel	Song of Solomon	Daniel
	1 Kings		Hosea
	2 Kings		Joel
	1 Chronicles		Amos
	2 Chronicles		Obadiah
	Ezra		Jonah
	Nehemiah		Micah
	Esther		Nahum
			Habakkuk
			Zephaniah
			Haggai
			Zechariah
			Malachi

The Old Testament was written between 1440 BC (before Christ) and about 400 BC. It is important to note that the Old

Testament is not necessarily organized in the chronological order in which they were written, but in the above order.

Why should you read the Old Testament today?

1. **Jesus taught the Old Testament is God's Word.**
   It is clear that Jesus and the New Testament writers believed the Old Testament tells God's message. Jesus spoke against the Pharisees because they cherished their traditions over the *"commandment of God"* in the Old Testament *(Matthew 15:3)*.

   Jesus also said, *"until heaven and earth pass away, not the smallest letter or stroke shall pass from the Law until all is accomplished" (Matthew 5:18)*. Paul also called the Old Testament, *"the Holy Scriptures which are able to make you wise for salvation through faith which is in Christ Jesus" (2 Timothy 3:15)*.

2. **To learn more about how God created His world.** One of the most important verses in the whole Bible is the first. *Genesis 1:1* tells us, *"In the beginning, God created the heavens and the earth."* All that we see, and all that we have, comes from God.

3. **To learn from the history of God's people.** When God's people were faithful, God blessed them. When they were not faithful, they suffered the results of their disobedience. As you learn the lessons and stories of the Old Testament, you will see how they apply to us, even today. **It is important to remember faithfulness to God may not result in material blessings. God's blessings occur in many forms.**

4. **To understand God's promises, blessings, and judgments. The Old Testament:**
   - Gives us many stories of people who learned to walk with God.

- Gives us wisdom from the very heart of God.
- Offers songs and poems that we can use to worship God today.
- Makes it clear that obeying God is not always easy but is required and expected for those who follow God.
- Points to the fulfilled promise we have in Jesus Christ.

Assignment for this Chapter: Lead a Discovery Bible Study from different parts of the Old Testament. Consider the following list if you need help choosing a passage.

1. God Creates *(Genesis 1:1-25)*
2. Man and Woman Eat the Fruit *(Genesis 3:1-13)*
3. God's Curses *(Genesis 3:14-24)*
4. God Saves Noah and His Family *(Genesis 6:9-8:14)*
5. God's Covenant with Noah *(Genesis 8:15-9:17)*
6. God's Covenant with Abram *(Genesis 12:1-8; 15:1-6; 17:1-7)*
7. Abraham Gives His Son as an Offering *(Genesis 22:1-19)*
8. God Saves His People *(Exodus 12:1-28)*
9. The Commands of God *(Exodus 20:1-21)*
10. God's Righteous Servant *(Isaiah 53)*

Continue sharing your story and God's story.

Chapter Journal

I will: _____

_____

_____

I will: _____

_____

_____

I will: _____

_____

_____

I will: _____

_____

_____

Notes:

_____

_____

_____

_____

Chapter 8
The Story of the Old Testament

Expected Outcome: Every disciple maker will learn and share the story of the Old Testament.

The Old Testament is filled with incredible stories of kings and nations, warriors and battles, shepherds and farmers, slavery and freedom, love and hate, prophesies and fulfillment. **All of these stories point to God's greatness and faithfulness in the lives of average men and women.** The Old Testament shows God's love, mercy, holiness, righteousness, and power.

There are over 300 prophecies (prophecy—a prediction of what will happen) about Jesus in the Old Testament, some of which were written 1,000 years before He came to the earth. **Without the Old Testament, the story of Christ is incomplete.** (For example, read or listen to *Acts 7* to understand how Stephen used the Old Testament to point others to Jesus.)

In *Acts 7:1-8*, Stephen talks about a man named Abraham whom God called to be the father of His chosen people (Israel). Most of the stories of the Old Testament talk about how God dealt with the people of Israel. The remainder of the Old Testament is the story of God's dealing with mankind. Ultimately, each story points to the need for a Savior (Jesus), who would one day pay the price for all the sins of the world. By taking our place on the cross, Jesus gives all who believe a chance to be restored to right relationship with God. Now, look at some of the most important Old Testament stories below.

Creation: (Read or listen to Genesis 1-2)
- God created the universe, the sky, the earth, the waters, the animals, and everything else.

- God made a perfect place on the earth called the Garden of Eden. He created the first man and named him Adam, and then placed him in the garden. He took a rib from Adam and created the first woman, named Eve.
- Adam and Eve were perfect and sinless, and the Lord walked in the garden with them.

The Fall of Mankind: (Genesis 3)
- Adam and Eve were given authority over all of God's creation but were told by God to not eat fruit from one specific tree called the "Tree of the Knowledge of Good and Evil."
- Satan (the leader of the angels who rebelled against God) came in the form of a snake and deceived Adam and Eve. They disobeyed God by eating the fruit.
- This disobedience towards God, known as "sin," created a separation in their relationship with God. They were removed from the Garden of Eden and God's presence. Adam and Eve's disobedience made the intimate relationship they once enjoyed with God impossible.
- God is perfectly holy and cannot tolerate even one sin. Without a Savior (Jesus) to forgive our sins and cleanse us of our unrighteousness, humanity has no way to be brought back into a right relationship with God. Only through the righteousness of Jesus could humanity be reconciled to God and return to His presence.

Group Discussion: How do you think it felt to be cast out of God's presence and direct relationship?

The Flood: (Genesis 6:5-9:28)
- After many generations, God saw how great mankind's wickedness was and grieved over it.
- God found one man who was righteous, named Noah. God commanded him to build a massive boat because He was going to send a flood to destroy all of His Creation on the earth.
- Noah, his three sons, and their wives, along with two of every kind of animal on the earth, entered the boat. It rained for 40 days and nights until the entire earth was covered with water.
- After more than a year on the boat, God caused the flood waters to return to normal, and Noah and his family left the boat.
- God put His rainbow in the sky to show His promise to never again flood the entire earth, for He is merciful to mankind.

Group Discussion: What examples do you have from your own life when God showed you mercy?

The Tower of Babel: (Genesis 11:1-9)
- After the flood, mankind continued in sin and became filled with pride.
- Humans wanted to show how great they were, so they came together to build a tower that would reach to the heavens.
- God stopped their plan by confusing their language so they could not work together.
- The confusion of the languages caused humanity to spread throughout the world, so they would not marvel at their works but instead become fruitful and multiply as God designed.

> **Key Principle:** Humanity continued to become more disobedient and unfaithful to God. Without a relationship with God, we will always choose to be disobedient and unfaithful to God.

The God of Abraham, Isaac, and Jacob: (Genesis 12-35)

Abraham: (Genesis 12-23)
- A few hundred years later, God made Himself known to a man named Abraham. God told him to leave his home on a journey where He would show him a land that would be given to him and his descendants.
- God brought him to the land that would eventually become the nation of Israel. Here, God made a covenant with Abraham that one day the Savior of the world would come through his descendants *(Matthew 1:17).*
- Abraham and his wife Sarah were very old and longed for children when the Lord spoke and promised them a son: Isaac.

Isaac: (Genesis 21:1-8; 25:19-26:34)
- God made a covenant with Isaac: through him and his descendants, the Savior would come.
- Isaac married Rebekah, but she was barren. The Lord opened her womb and she had twins, Jacob and Esau. Esau was the older and Jacob was the younger. The Lord told Rebekah before they were born that the older would serve the younger.
- These two brothers were the fathers of two nations, Edom and Israel. The two nations fought and battled for hundreds of years.

Jacob: (Genesis 25:21-34; 27- 35)
- Jacob deceived Esau, his brother, into giving up his birthright as the firstborn son. Then, he tricked his

father, Isaac, into giving him the blessings that were meant for the eldest son.
- An angel came to Jacob while he was sleeping, and they wrestled through the night. Because of this encounter, Jacob became a changed man, and the angel changed Jacob's name to Israel.
- Israel had 12 sons, and they became the 12 tribes of Israel.

Key Principle: God's timing is not always our timing. Abraham, Isaac, and Jacob spent much of their lives waiting for God to fulfill His promises to them. Some of those promises were fulfilled in the lives of their descendants.

The 12 Tribes of Israel: (Genesis 35:23-26)
- These are the sons of Israel in order of their birth: Reuben, Simeon, Levi, Judah, Dan, Naphtali, Gad, Asher, Issachar, Zebulun, Joseph, and Benjamin.
- The tribes kept the names of their specific forefathers and were all given a different territory within the land of Israel.
- Jesus came through the descendants of Judah, which was prophesied in the Old Testament *(Genesis 49:10; Isaiah 11:1-5).*

Moses and the Egyptians: (The Book of Exodus)
- Many years later, Abraham's descendants were enslaved for 400 years by the Egyptians. God heard their cry and rose up a leader.
- When Moses was born, there was an order from the Pharaoh (leader) of Egypt to kill any baby boys who were born to Israelites. To save his life, Moses' mother put him in a river in a basket. The daughter of the Pharaoh of Egypt found Moses and adopted him *(Exodus 2:1-10).*
- Moses grew up in the household of the Pharaoh for 40 years. One day, he saw an Egyptian guard beating an

- Israelite, so Moses killed the guard. Moses ran and hid for 40 years in the desert of Midian *(Exodus 2:11-23)*.
- One day while walking in the mountains, Moses saw a bush that was on fire but not burning up. The Lord spoke to him through this bush and told him that He would use Moses to set the Israelites free *(Exodus 3:1-4:14)*.
- Moses went to Pharaoh and asked him to release the Israelites. Pharaoh refused, so God sent ten plagues to the land of Egypt to display His power and judge their gods.
- The Israelites were freed from Egypt, but Pharaoh changed his mind. When the Israelites reached the Red Sea, the Egyptian army caught up to them. With nowhere to go, the Lord told Moses to raise his staff above the waters. The Lord split the Red Sea and the Israelites walked across on dry ground. When the Egyptians tried to cross, the sea came crashing down and killed the entire Egyptian army *(Exodus 12:31-42; 14:1-31)*.
- Moses led the Israelites through the desert for 40 years *(Exodus 12:37)*. God provided bread from the sky called "manna." They wandered until they came to the land promised to Abraham, Isaac, and Jacob. It was occupied by a people called the Canaanites *(Numbers 14:1-20; Exodus 16:35)*.
- Hundreds of years before Moses and the Israelites approached the land of Canaan, God promised to give this land to their ancestors Abraham *(Genesis 15:18-21)*, Isaac *(Genesis 26:2-5)*, and Jacob *(Genesis 28:10-15)*.
- The land God promised to the Israelites was very good and had enough water and space for farming and raising animals *(Numbers 14:6-8)*.
- Moses never entered the promised land because he disobeyed God. Instead, Joshua would lead the Israelites the rest of the journey *(Deuteronomy 32:48-52)*.

Group Discussion: What captures your attention as you hear all the things that happened in the book of Exodus? How does Moses' example of faithfulness and obedience encourage you to pursue God?

Joshua the Warrior: (The Book of Joshua)
- Joshua was a strong warrior, a great leader, and fully devoted to God. He was mentored by Moses.
- Joshua led the Israelites into their promised land. They conquered much of the land around them and were feared throughout the region, though they failed to take control of the whole region God had promised to them.
- Under his leadership, they divided Israel into different territories and gave one to each of the 12 tribes of Israel.

The Judges: (Judges; 1 Samuel 1-8)
- When Israel first became a nation, they had no king. God was their ruler and their leader.
- Whenever neighboring countries would rise up and try to destroy Israel, God would raise up a leader. They were referred to as the "Judges," or may even be seen as "tribal chiefs."
- God also used priests and prophets to rule Israel, like Eli and Samuel *(1 Samuel 4:3; 7:3-16)*.

The Kings: (1 Samuel 8-1 Kings 1)
- Instead of continuing to have God as their king, Israel rebelled and asked Samuel for a human king like the nations around them. Through the prophet Samuel, God warned them that the king would fail, but they refused to listen.

Israel's First King: Saul (1 Samuel 8-31)
- Saul was a tall, strong man whom God anointed to be king.

- At first, Saul won many battles and served the Lord. The nation was united under his leadership.
- Eventually, Saul became proud and no longer followed the Lord. The Lord rejected Saul as king and chose David to be his replacement.

A King after God's Own Heart: David (1 Samuel 16 – 1 Kings 1)

- David was a shepherd boy when Saul was king, the youngest son in his family *(1 Samuel 17:14)*.
- One day, the prophet Samuel was sent by God to anoint David as the future king of Israel *(1 Samuel 16:12-13)*.
- In this time, there was a long-standing war between Israel and the Philistines. The Philistines had a giant warrior named Goliath whom no Israelite would fight. Hearing Goliath speak against the God of Israel, David, who was not old enough to serve in the military, volunteered to fight him. David defeated Goliath with a sling and a stone and instantly became the hero of Israel.
- King Saul became jealous and tried to kill David for many years. He chased David all throughout the wilderness of Israel in order to kill him. Eventually, Saul died in battle.
- David was made king. The Lord promised that the Savior of the world (Jesus) would come through David's offspring. David was one of Judah's descendants, which fulfilled the prophecies made about Jesus.

The Wise King of Israel: Solomon (1 Kings 1- 11)

- The second son of David and Bathsheba, Solomon was anointed as the next king of Israel *(1 Kings 1:28-39)*.
- Solomon was blessed by God with great wisdom, power, and wealth. He ruled over Israel as its richest and most successful king. Some of the books in the Old Testament like Proverbs, Ecclesiastes, and the Song of

- Solomon were likely written by Solomon *(1 Kings 3:4-15; 4:20-34)*.
- During his reign as king, Solomon built the first Temple in Jerusalem. It was a beautiful and extravagant building where the Jews worshiped God *(1 Kings 6)*.
- Even though Solomon was richly blessed with wisdom, power, and wealth, he eventually worshiped the false gods his wives worshiped *(1 Kings 11:1-13)*.
- Solomon's disobedience and his unfaithfulness to God led to the splitting of the nation of Israel. Israel would never again possess the land, riches, or strength it had during the reign of Solomon.

Group Discussion: Are there any warnings you see in God's Word that you are ignoring or not following in obedience? Consider what happened in the lives of the people throughout the Old Testament who heard God's instructions but failed to listen. Spend time in prayer and reflection to see how God is speaking to you now. Respond in obedience!

Divided Kingdom - Israel and Judah: (1 Kings 12)
- When Solomon's son, Rehoboam, was made king, half the nation rejected him and named their own king. The nation of Israel split into two separate nations: **Israel** and **Judah**.
- After they divided, both had many kings over a few hundred years. Most did evil in the eyes of the Lord.
- Both of these nations were eventually conquered: Israel was exiled to Assyria and Judah to Babylon.

Conquered - Babylon, Persia, Greece, Rome: (2 Kings 17-25)
- After a time of exile, both nations eventually returned to their homeland.
- The next few hundred years, the known world was conquered by different empires. One would conquer the other, and world power was passed on to the next.

They each ruled over Israel and Judah at some point in time.
- During this time, God sent many prophets to get His people's attention. Their messages are now some of the books of the Old Testament.
- Prophets like Hosea and Jeremiah wrote the words God gave them to speak to confront the nation of Israel for its unfaithfulness *(Hosea 4:1-3; Jeremiah 36:2).*
- Prophets like Obadiah and Ezekiel pronounced God's judgment on the idolatrous nations that surrounded Israel *(Obadiah 1:1-4; Ezekiel 25:1-7).*
- Other prophets, like Elijah and Jonah, were directly involved in leading others to obedience in God through miraculous signs and acts *(1 Kings 18:20-40; Jonah 3:1-10).*

Songs and Wisdom: Job, Psalms, Proverbs, Ecclesiastes, Song of Solomon, and Lamentations

The Old Testament contains a collection of songs, proverbs, and wisdom literature. These are tools to edify, comfort, instruct, exhort, and correct the people of God.

400 Years of Silence: (Malachi 4)
- Malachi was the last prophet of the Old Testament.
- In Malachi's writing, God says that He would send a prophet like Elijah to be the predecessor for the Messiah.
- John the Baptist was sent with the spirit of Elijah as the predecessor to the Lord Jesus 400 years after Malachi.

A New Beginning
- Christ is found throughout the Old Testament. He is the central message of the Scriptures.
- Jesus is the bridge between the two testaments. In the Old Testament, God's focus is the covenant He made with the Israelites. Through Christ, God has made a

new covenant with mankind. This is the full story, and through Christ, we have a new beginning.
- Consider the chart on the following page to better understand how the Old Testament predicted the arrival and ministry of Jesus in the New Testament. Knowing and reading the Old Testament prepares you to better understand the work and life of Jesus in the New Testament.

	Old Testament Prophecy	New Testament Fulfillment
Law	*"All nations will be blessed through you" (Genesis 12:3).* God tells Abraham he will have a son, even though he and his wife are old *(Genesis 17:15-16).*	Jesus is a descendant of Abraham. He is the blessing to all the nations through his death and resurrection.
History	Ruth's husband dies, and Boaz, a relative of her husband, redeems her by marrying her and taking her under his protection *(Ruth 4:9-22).*	Jesus is a descendant of Ruth and Boaz, who is our kinsman redeemer *(Matthew 1:5-6).*
Poetry & Wisdom	*"They divide my garments among them, and for my clothing they cast lots"* *(Psalm 22:18).*	During the crucifixion, the Roman soldiers ripped Jesus' garments and cast lots to see who would take Jesus' possessions *(Luke 23:34).*
Prophets	*"The Lord himself will give you a sign. Behold, the virgin shall conceive and bear a son, and shall call his name Immanuel [which means 'God is with us']"* *(Isaiah 7:14).*	Jesus is conceived of the Holy Spirit, born of the virgin Mary *(Matthew 1:18).*

Assignment for this Chapter: Every point that is throughout this chapter represents an incredible story to study, learn from, and share with others. Listening or reading through each book of the Old Testament in its entirety will greatly help you understand the full story of the Bible. An Old Testament reading guide is included at the end of this book to keep track of your progress in reading the whole Old Testament.

Share one powerful story from the Old Testament this week with someone you know.

Chapter Journal

I will: _____

_____

_____

I will: _____

_____

_____

I will: _____

_____

_____

I will: _____

_____

_____

Notes:

_____

_____

_____

_____

Chapters 9-10
Trainer's Guide

⬅ Look Back

Give everyone a chance to share, hear from others, and be held accountable. Focus on encouragement, celebration, and following through with assignments.
- Have <u>everyone</u> report back on how they shared their story, God's story, and followed through with what they said they would do since the last training.
- Discuss how you have put into practice the things you have learned from the Old Testament.
- Did you share any stories from the Old Testament with anyone? How did they receive it? Spend some time celebrating the victories you are experiencing and also praying for those who are struggling.

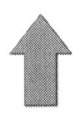

⬆ Look Up

Chapters 9-10 focus on the New Testament and, specifically, the life and ministry of Jesus. There is an extra amount of Scripture references and quotes in Chapter 10. Make sure you do not skip over these very important verses. It is critical that you focus on the following as you train through this chapter:
- What Jesus valued, how He spent his time, how He lived, and what He expects from those who follow Him.
- How Jesus' life, death, and resurrection provide forgiveness from death and sin, guarantee salvation to all who believe, and put us into a loving relationship with God.
- Notice especially how Jesus treated people throughout His life, even those who harassed and persecuted Him.
- **Remember to highlight the expected outcome and key principle!** Encourage memorization of key Scripture verses.
- **Hearing from God:** At the end of each chapter, allow for a time of silent prayer and reflection, specifically looking for what each person should do in response to God speaking to their heart.

Group Activity: Help each disciple maker create a one-page summary of the Gospel in their own words. Focus on the main points in the life, death, and resurrection of Jesus. From this, prepare an easy to remember message, sermon, or lesson that can be used to train others.

Model & Practice: Every trainer should share practical ways the life and words of Jesus have transformed their lives.

Look Forward

Before moving on to the assignment for the week, ask the following questions:
- How is God speaking to your heart today?
- How is God calling you to greater obedience?
- What will you do today & this week in response to God's voice?

Assignment for this Chapter:
- Carefully read or listen to each of the Gospels to become familiar with Jesus' life, words, miracles, and teachings. Share what you learn about Jesus with someone this week.
- Make a list of 10 verses to begin memorizing from the Gospels. These can include statements Jesus made, important principles to begin practicing, and anything else that can be used to encourage those you are discipling.
- Write your I will statement(s) in the chapter journal.

Chapter 9
The Story of the New Testament

Expected Outcome: Every disciple maker will learn and share the story of the New Testament.

Introduction to the New Testament

The New Testament is the story of Jesus Christ and the salvation that comes through Him. It also talks about the birth of the church, its growth in the 1st century, and the teachings the apostles gave to the early church for its unity, maturity, and expansion. It closes with the message about the future of Christ's Kingdom.

There are 27 books in the New Testament written over a 50-year period by Jesus' apostles, disciples, and followers. The first four books in the New Testament are called the Gospels, which means "Good News." These four books focus on Jesus' life, ministry, death, and resurrection.

The rest of the New Testament books introduce the birth and expansion of the church. They also include instructional and corrective letters written to church leaders, and prophecies of Jesus' return and the reign and rule of His Kingdom on earth as it is in heaven. All of these books are rich in encouragement and help us better understand who God is and what He expects of His followers. Reading (or listening), understanding, applying, and training others in the New Testament is vital for every disciple maker's spiritual growth *(2 Peter 1:3; 2 Timothy 2:2)*.

Just as the Old Testament contains different types of writings, the New Testament is also a collection of different kinds of writing. It is important to remember the different types (or genres) of writing. This understanding will help you better interpret what you are reading. The three types of writing in the New Testament are narrative, letters, and prophecy.

Narrative: Matthew, Mark, Luke, and John record the life of Christ, and Acts tells the story of the early church and the spread of the Gospel.

Letters: The letters are divided into two categories: **Paul's Letters** and **General Letters** (see chart below). Paul's letters are the ones written by Paul, while the general letters were written by other church leaders. Most of these letters were written to individual churches or leaders across the growing New Testament church.

Prophecy: The Book of Revelation stands alone in the New Testament. In this book, there are many visions, symbols, and images that picture God's actions in the future.

Narrative	Paul's Letters	General Letters	Prophecy
Matthew	Romans	Hebrews	Revelation
Mark	1 & 2 Corinthians	James	
Luke	Galatians	1 & 2 Peter	
John	Ephesians	1, 2, & 3 John	
Acts	Philippians	Jude	
	Colossians		
	1 & 2 Thessalonians		
	1 & 2 Timothy		
	Titus		
	Philemon		

Key Principle: Understanding the type of book you are reading in the New Testament will help you correctly interpret and apply the Scriptures to your life.

Order of the New Testament

Just like the Old Testament, the individual books and letters of the New Testament were written by multiple authors under the leading of the Holy Spirit (Matthew, Mark, Luke, John, Paul, Peter, James, Jude). There is no God-given order for the way the books are arranged. For example, the letters written by Paul are organized according to their length as opposed to the dates they were written. With this in mind, consider the following points that highlight the order in which the New Testament was written.

1. Peter, Paul, and other leaders in the early church wrote letters to the churches they planted during the events recorded in the Book of Acts. Some of these letters are included in the New Testament.

2. Some books in the New Testament were written around the same time.

3. Some of the Gospels were written after the events in the Book of Acts happened.

It is difficult to know the exact date each of the books were written. For this reason, the table below shows a generally accepted range of years each book was written.

James	AD 40-50	*2 Peter*	AD 60-68
Galatians	AD 49-50	*Luke/Acts*	AD 63-64
1 Thessalonians	AD 49	*1 Timothy*	AD 64-67
2 Thessalonians	AD 49	*Titus*	AD 64-67
Matthew	AD 50-64	*Hebrews*	AD 64-70
Ephesians	AD 50-51	*2 Timothy*	AD 64-67
Philippians	AD 50-51	*Mark*	AD 65-70
Colossians	AD 50-51	*Jude*	AD 65-80
Philemon	AD 50-51	*John*	AD 80-95
Romans	AD 57-59	*1 John*	AD 90-100
1 Corinthians	AD 57	*2 John*	AD 90-100
2 Corinthians	AD 57	*3 John*	AD 90-100
1 Peter	AD 58-68	*Revelation*	AD 90-95

Chapter 10
The Life & Ministry of Jesus

Expected Outcome: Every disciple maker will model their life and ministry after the life and ministry of Jesus.

When Adam and Eve sinned in the Garden of Eden, humanity was removed from the presence of God, and their direct relationship with Him separated. Humanity needed a Savior. God gave the Israelites a system of laws and sacrifices, but none of these things could save them. Everything pointed to the coming Messiah—Jesus, the Savior of the world.

Jesus' Preparation for Ministry

In the last book of the Old Testament *(Malachi),* God said that He would send a prophet to be the one to announce the coming of the Savior *(Malachi 3:1).* This prophet was John the Baptist, Jesus' cousin. People came from great distances to hear John preach. John made it clear that he was not the Savior but that he was only preparing the way for Jesus *(Luke 1:19-34).*

The supernatural birth of Jesus was prophesied by multiple prophets in the Old Testament. (See charts in Chapter 10.) Mary, the mother of Jesus, was engaged to be married to a man named Joseph, but Joseph was not the father of Jesus. Jesus was conceived by the Holy Spirit and born to Mary even though she was a virgin *(Matthew 1:18-20).* Jesus' virgin birth was the beginning of a new phase of God's activity among humanity. Unlike everyone born before Him, Jesus' body was not cursed by the sin Adam and Eve passed to their children.

During this time, Herod, the ruler over Israel, heard that a king had been born. As a result, he ordered every boy in Bethlehem 2 years old or younger be killed *(Matthew 2:16-*

18). However, an angel told Joseph in a dream to leave Bethlehem, so he took Mary and Jesus and fled to Egypt to avoid Herod's murderous act *(Matthew 2:13-15)*.

The childhood of Jesus is not well known. The Scriptures provide little information about His childhood, but what we need to know about what Jesus accomplished when He was an adult is incredibly detailed. We do know that Luke records the story of when Jesus was brought to Jerusalem for one of the important festivals. On their return trip, Mary and Joseph realized that Jesus was not with them. When they found Jesus, then just 12 years old, He was talking with the teachers in the Temple and amazing them with His words. Jesus' divine wisdom and special connection to God the Father were already observable by the people he encountered.

When Jesus reached adulthood, followed in His earthly father Joseph's profession as a carpenter in Nazareth. Jesus started His public ministry at the age of 30.

The Baptism of Jesus

One day, Jesus approached John the Baptist (who was baptizing people), requesting that he baptize Him. (John was known as John the Baptizer and was sent for the purpose of announcing the coming of Jesus as the Messiah.) John recognized who Jesus was and said, *"You should baptize me!"* Jesus convinced John that it was fulfilling God's plan for John to baptize Him. After John baptized Jesus, the Holy Spirit came in the form of a dove, and a declaration came from Heaven, saying, *"This is my beloved Son, with whom I am well pleased" (See Matthew 3:13-17)*.

Key Principle: Jesus set an example for us to follow. Baptism is a public declaration of our faith and association with Jesus. It is identifying with His death, burial, and resurrection. Before He preached a sermon or worked a miracle, Jesus was first baptized. His baptism introduced Him and His ministry to the people of Israel. When you are baptized, you are likewise introducing yourself to those around you as a follower of Christ. It is the first act of obedience for a new believer.

Action Step: Are you baptized? If not, follow the example and command of Jesus and be baptized.

The Temptation of Jesus

The ministry of Jesus officially started when John baptized Him. The Holy Spirit then led Jesus into the wilderness where Satan tried to tempt Jesus to sin *(Matthew 4)*. Jesus spent forty days and nights fasting. Even though Jesus was suffering from the hunger and thirst of His human body, He demonstrated His spiritual strength by resisting the temptations of Satan.

Group Discussion: After forty days of fasting, Jesus was naturally hungry. Even though He was weak and hungry, Jesus did not dishonor His Father by falling for the temptations of Satan. Jesus was able to resist the devil's temptations because He was in deep communion with His Father. How can you follow the example of Jesus and resist temptations?

The Beginning of the Work: Jesus' First Year of Ministry

With Jesus' time of preparation complete, He began His first full year of ministry. During this first year, Jesus began to do miracles before the people and started to share the focus of His message: *"Repent, for the kingdom of heaven is at hand" (Matthew 4:17)*.

Jesus spent most of this first year by the Jordan River in a small region known as Judea. He experienced His first rejection in His hometown. From there, He proceeded north along the Jordan River to a region known as Capernaum where He chose most of His disciples. Most teachers at that time selected the best and brightest students, but Jesus chose the local, uneducated people to carry His message.

Group Discussion: How does it feel to know that the people Jesus recruited to expand the ministry were not the best and smartest but the untrained people who were willing to faithfully follow Him?

Matthew, Mark, and Luke do not describe most of what happened in Jesus' first year of ministry, and even John only covers a small amount. However, this time was not a period of inactivity. Jesus traveled throughout Galilee teaching, preaching, and healing. He was often followed by large groups of people and became well-known in the region. Many people followed Him, but most were there to see His miracles or to receive healing from Him, not to truly serve Him.

By the end of Jesus' first year of public ministry, there must have been a feeling of excitement in Galilee. Word began to spread widely that a miracle worker had appeared in Israel.

Jesus was clear that He only taught what He received from His Father *(John 7:16)*. Jesus knew the inner truths of the Kingdom of God and He shared them with His closest followers. While He shared these things with His disciples, He strictly forbid them from telling the crowds that He was the Messiah *(Luke 9:18-21)*. If the people knew that Jesus was the Messiah, they would have tried to make Him king, but this was not part of God's plan.

Jesus told His disciples, *"The Son of Man must suffer many things, and be rejected by the elders, and chief priests, and scribes, and be killed, and be raised" (Luke 9:22)*. Jesus was not the Messiah the people expected, but He was the only One who could save humanity.

With such an exciting beginning, Jesus' ministry was about to enter its period of greatest popularity. One story from this period describes the interaction between Jesus and a religious leader.

One day, Jesus was teaching religious leaders in a house. His reputation was growing as a great healer. Four men heard Him speaking and remembered their paralyzed friend. When they brought their friend to the house where Jesus was speaking, it was too crowded to go inside. The men climbed up onto the roof, made a hole in it, and lowered their friend down on his bed.

Seeing their faith, Jesus turned His attention to the paralyzed man. Jesus told the man, "Take heart my son, your sins are forgiven." Some of the religious leaders there questioned how Jesus could say such a thing. After all, who can forgive sins but God alone? Jesus responded to their thoughts and said, "Which is easier, to say your sins are forgiven or rise and walk?" But so that they would know that the Son of Man has authority on Earth, He said, "Rise, pick up your mattress and go home." Instantly the paralyzed man stood up and was healed! When the crowd saw this act of power, they praised God and marveled at Jesus, saying they had never seen anything like this before (Matthew 9:1-8; Mark 2:1-12; Luke 5:17-26).

The Time of Popularity: Jesus' Second Year of Ministry

Starting His second year of ministry, Jesus faced increased challenges and pressure from the religious leaders who felt threatened by Him. These leaders thought He violated their rules about what could and couldn't be done on the Sabbath (the weekly Jewish holy day).

This added to the disapproval they felt for Jesus. An important event during the second year was Jesus' "Sermon on the

Mount." This message was given to clarify the true nature of righteousness and God's Kingdom *(Matthew 5-7)*.

Jesus confirmed the prophet Micah's emphasis—God desires justice, kindness, and walking humbly with Him *(Micah 6:6-8)*. Jesus clearly showed the difference between true righteousness and the rituals and religion the Jewish religious leaders considered most important. Jesus' message and teachings caused difficulty for the religious leaders because Jesus was rejecting their entire system of thinking and encouraging the people to think and act differently too.

Jesus traveled around Galilee, performing many miracles showing He was the Son of God. The religious leaders tried to explain these miracles as demonic or Satan-inspired. Responding to this serious charge, Jesus began using parables in His teaching. These parables were simple and memorable stories used to teach the listener a timeless spiritual truth or lesson.

During this time, John the Baptist was killed for speaking out against the sin of Herod, the king of the Jews *(Mark 6:27)*. Shortly afterward, Jesus miraculously fed a crowd of thousands and gained so much approval that the people wanted to make Him king *(John 6:15)*. Despite this honor and acceptance, it would soon become clear that the people did not want to follow Jesus as their king.

Group Discussion: What extraordinary things our Lord could do! When God walked among human beings He healed, taught, and did amazing works! What amazing things have you seen Jesus do in your life or community?

As Jesus became more vocal against the unrighteousness and pride of the religious leaders, His opposition increased, and popularity decreased. This led Him closer to His greatest work of all: His sacrifice on the cross. Consider and discuss one story from this period.

One day, Jesus preached to a large crowd of people. As time passed, many people were hungry. The disciples approached Jesus, requesting that He send them away to eat. Jesus responded by asking them, "Why don't you feed them?" They were unable to do this, of course. Andrew, one of Jesus' disciples, brought one boy with five loaves of bread and two fish. Jesus had the disciples divide the crowd into groups of 50 and then sit down. Jesus took the bread and fish, blessed it, and gave it to the disciples to distribute to the crowd of 5,000 men. The entire crowd ate their fill and when they were finished, there were 12 baskets leftover. (See Matthew 14:13-21 for the whole story.)

The Time of Rejection: Jesus' Third Year of Ministry

During Jesus' third year of ministry, things became more difficult. The religious leaders were more determined than ever to persecute Him. Meanwhile, some of the ordinary people turned against Him as well. None of this stopped Jesus, but it did lead Him to make changes in His ministry.

"He came to his own people, and even they rejected him" (John 1:11). Jesus would not force Himself on anyone. Whenever He was rejected in one town or city, He went on to the next place.

Group Discussion: When Jesus faced difficulty, He did not stop His work. He made changes in order to fulfill the task He had been given by God. How can you better handle opposition and challenges?

Twice, Jesus escaped death in Jerusalem. His time had not yet come, but the moment He would be handed over to be crucified was approaching, and He knew it. Jesus spoke clearly with His disciples about His upcoming death at the hands of the religious leaders *(Matthew 26:1-5)*. In the final year of Jesus' ministry, it was clear that He was committed to fulfilling His Father's plan of providing salvation for all mankind for all ages, no matter the cost.

Read and discuss the following story told by Jesus: *(John 10:1-21)*

"Most assuredly, I say to you, he who does not enter the sheepfold by the door, but climbs up some other way, the same is a thief and a robber. But he who enters by the door is the shepherd of the sheep. To him the doorkeeper opens, and the sheep hear his voice; and he calls his own sheep by name and leads them out. And when he brings out his own sheep, he goes before them; and the sheep follow him, for they know his voice. Yet they will by no means follow a stranger, but will flee from him, for they do not know the voice of strangers." Jesus used this illustration, but they did not understand the things which He spoke to them.

Then Jesus said to them again, "Most assuredly, I say to you, I am the door of the sheep. All who ever came before Me are thieves and robbers, but the sheep did not hear them. I am the door. If anyone enters by Me, he will be saved, and will go in and out and find pasture. The thief does not come except to steal, and to kill, and to destroy. I have come that they may have life, and that they may have it more abundantly.

"I am the good shepherd. The good shepherd gives His life for the sheep. But a hireling, he who is not the shepherd, one who does not own the sheep, sees the wolf coming and leaves the sheep and flees; and the wolf catches the sheep and scatters them. The hireling flees because he is a hireling and does not care about the sheep. I am the good shepherd; and I know My sheep, and am known by My own. As the Father knows Me, even so I know the Father; and I lay down My life for the sheep. And other sheep I have which are not of this fold; them also I must bring, and they will hear My voice; and there will

be one flock and one shepherd. "Therefore My Father loves Me, because I lay down My life that I may take it again. No one takes it from Me, but I lay it down of Myself. I have power to lay it down, and I have power to take it again. This command I have received from My Father."

Therefore there was a division again among the Jews because of these sayings. And many of them said, "He has a demon and is mad. Why do you listen to Him?" Others said, "These are not the words of one who has a demon. Can a demon open the eyes of the blind?"

The Path Towards the Cross: Jesus' Fourth Year of Ministry

Jesus' fourth year of ministry marked the beginning of the end: He made his way toward Jerusalem and the cross. Over the course of the year, He prepared His followers for what was going to happen and began finishing up His public ministry.

As Jesus headed towards Jerusalem to meet His death, He instructed His disciples, challenged the crowds, invited them to follow Him, and confronted the religious leadership. He prepared the disciples for what would happen in the near future and the ministry they would serve after He was gone *(John 16:1-33)*. Jesus gave the crowds more opportunities to respond as He showed the way of the current religious leaders was not the way of God.

Jesus focused on preparing His disciples for what would soon happen. By February of AD 33, Jesus was in Jericho, more than 15 miles from Jerusalem. From Jericho, where Jesus healed a blind man and led a tax collector to faith, Jesus departed for Jerusalem *(Luke 18:35-43; 19:1-10)*. He chose the time of Passover (a Jewish festival celebrating Israel's deliverance from Egypt) to make His final entry into the city.

While Jesus was busy teaching in one place, the disciples received word that their friend Lazarus was very sick and requested that Jesus come to him. Jesus did not go immediately but waited two days. Jesus said to the disciples, "It is good for you that we were not there so that the Son of God may be glorified before you." When they arrived, Lazarus' sisters ran to Jesus and told Him that Lazarus had died. They said, "If only You had come, Lazarus would not have died." Jesus said that Lazarus was not dead but was sleeping. Jesus then requested that they go to the place he was buried. Jesus wept and the people said, "Look at how much He loved him!" Jesus told them to remove the stone from the grave. Although the people warned Him that it would smell, Jesus assured them that everything was fine. Jesus prayed, gave thanks to the Father, and said "Lazarus, come out" Immediately, Lazarus came out of the tomb! The people were amazed, for the man that was dead was alive and came out! (See John 11:1-44 for the whole story.)

The Final Week

The term "Passion" is used to describe Jesus' sufferings and death. It is no surprise that each of the Gospels gives more attention to this time than to any other part of Jesus' story. This is where Jesus fulfilled His mission. This is where He completed the work of salvation for all who believe and trust in Him. **In His crucifixion and resurrection is where He confirms the victory over sin, Satan, death, and the grave.**

The following chart is a short summary of Jesus' final week:

Sunday	Jesus enters Jerusalem with rejoicing (Palm Sunday).	*Matt. 21:6-9*
Monday	Jesus curses a fig tree & cleanses the Temple.	*Matt. 21:12-22*
Tuesday	Jesus' authority is questioned, and He teaches in the Temple.	*Luke 20:1-8*
Wednesday	Jesus' enemies plot against Him.	*Matt. 26:3-5*
Thursday	Jesus shares the Last Supper with His disciples and prays in the Garden of Gethsemane.	*Mark 14:17-25; Matt 26:36-46*
Friday	Jesus is betrayed, arrested, tried, crucified and buried.	*Luke 22:47-23:55*
Saturday	Jesus' body remains in the tomb.	*Luke 23:56*
Sunday	Jesus rises from the dead!	*John 20:1-31*

Below is the most wonderful story ever told! Read or listen to this carefully, commit it to memory, and share with all you know!

As Jesus came to His last week of earthly ministry, He entered Jerusalem. On Thursday night Jesus and the disciples gathered together. Jesus wanted to tell the disciples what was about to happen, as this would be their last time together. During the meal, Jesus washed the feet of each of His disciples. This was a common practice for servants to wash the feet of a guest, but never by a master and leader. After He finished washing their feet, they had a meal together. During the meal Jesus took bread, blessed it, and gave it to the disciples saying, "Take, eat, this is My body which is given for you." He also took a cup of wine and when He had given thanks said, "Drink of it, all of you, for this is my blood, the covenant which is poured out for many; do this in remembrance of me." Though the disciples did not understand what this meal represented, it was a significant event that was the beginning of the Lord's Supper. (See John 13:1-17 and Luke 22:7-20 for the whole story.)

After dinner they walked to a nearby garden. Jesus asked the disciples to join Him in prayer as He was troubled and anticipated His coming death. Some of the religious leaders had already been plotting to kill Him. They had a secret plan with one of Jesus' disciples called Judas Iscariot. Judas Iscariot brought the religious leaders and guards to arrest Jesus. The disciples scattered in fear and Jesus was arrested and taken to the house of the High Priest. He was mocked and ridiculed. He was taken to different political leaders, but they could not find any fault in Him. Even the governor said, "This man has done nothing wrong."

As the news of Jesus' arrest spread, the crowds grew around the place that Jesus was held. The religious leaders enticed the crowds and encouraged them to demand that Jesus be crucified. Due to the pressure from the crowds, the governor (named Pilate) was forced to declare Jesus would be crucified. The guards stripped Him, beat Him, whipped Him, spit on Him, mocked Him, and made Him carry a cross through the city to the place where He would be crucified.

Jesus was taken to a place called Golgotha and was crucified between two criminals. They drove two nails into His hands and one nail between His feet to hold Him to the cross. As Jesus was on the cross, He asked the Father to forgive the people who were killing Him. Finally, Jesus gave up His life, breathed His last breath, and died. One soldier came and pierced His side to make sure He was really dead; and then He was buried in a new tomb according to what was prophesied about Him.

The religious leaders asked to seal the tomb where Jesus was buried, as Jesus had predicted His resurrection earlier. They also posted guards at the tomb to make sure that no one attempted to steal His body. Early Sunday morning, three days after Jesus was crucified, a powerful earthquake took place. The stone was removed, and Jesus resurrected from the dead!

He then appeared to His disciples and other followers for many days. He encouraged them to be witnesses of what they had seen and heard, and to tell others! Finally, in the presence of many followers, he ascended to Heaven and promised to return the same way. Just before leaving them, He told the disciples to wait in Jerusalem until He sent His Holy Spirit to empower them for the task ahead of them! (See Matthew 26-28 and Luke 24 for the complete story.)

Group Discussion: Jesus took the punishment we deserved so that we could be forgiven and have an eternal relationship with God. It was our sin that sent Jesus to the cross. This was all in accordance with God's divine plan to deliver humanity from the curse of their sin and bring them back into His presence. How does this make you feel? What is your response to this story today?

Group Activity: Help each disciple maker create a one-page summary of the Gospel in their own words. Focus on the main points in the life, death, and resurrection of Jesus. From this, prepare an easy to remember message, sermon, or lesson that can be used to train others.

Jesus' Work Completed

Jesus offers freedom from sin and death to all who by faith receive Him as their personal Savior. Entering God's Kingdom comes only by spiritual birth, a work of the Holy Spirit, as one receives this gift of God's Son *(John 3)*.

The resurrection not only means that Jesus is alive and that there is life after death, but also that He has proven to be who He claimed to be. God the Father has exalted Jesus into His presence in Heaven *(Philippians 2:9-11)*. On the day of Pentecost, God poured out His Holy Spirit upon all who believe in Jesus *(Acts 2:1-4)*. The Holy Spirit is now the companion, comforter, and guide for all believers today.

Jesus reigns this very day in Heaven. It is Jesus, the risen and exalted Savior, that the four Gospels tell all about. It is this Jesus we worship and proclaim to the world.

Group Discussion: How can you keep this wonderful story all to yourself? Should you keep quiet about this story? Who can you share this amazing love story with?

Action Step: Write down 10 names with whom you can go and share this story:

1. _____

2. _____

3. _____

4. _____

5. _____

6. _____

7. _____

8. _____

9. _____

10. _____

Assignment for this Chapter: Carefully read or listen to each of the Gospels to become familiar with Jesus' life, words, miracles, and teachings. Share what you learn about Jesus with someone this week. After reading all of the Gospels, continue with the Book of Acts and the rest of the New Testament. A New Testament reading guide is included at the end of this book to keep track of your reading progress.

Try to memorize the following written and visual illustration about the life of Jesus.

The Life of Jesus

1. An angel told Mary that, by the power of the Holy Spirit, she would conceive a son *(Luke 1:30-35)*.
2. She would name Him Jesus, and He would be the Son of God *(Luke 1:31)*.
3. When Jesus grew up, He started his ministry *(Luke 3:23)*.
4. He was baptized *(Luke 3:21)*.
5. He called disciples to join Him *(Luke 5:1-11)*.
6. He performed miracles, like healing the sick *(Mark 2:1-12)*,
7. He raised the dead *(John 11:40-46)*.
8. He taught people about His Father *(John 14:9-11)*.
9. It seemed like everyone loved Jesus *(Matthew 7:28-29)*.
10. But some people did not. They wanted Jesus to die *(Matthew 12:14)*.
11. They falsely accused Him *(Luke 23:1-5)*.
12. He was crucified and died *(Matthew 27:33-56)*.
13. He was buried *(Luke 23:50-56)*.
14. After 3 days, He rose from the dead *(Luke 24:1-9)*!
15. He appeared to His disciples and many others *(Luke 24:36)*.
16. He told His disciples to tell everyone His story *(Matthew 28:19-20)*.
17. He ascended into Heaven *(Acts 1:9)*.
18. He will return and take those who believe to be with Him *(John 14:3)*.

The Life of Jesus

Chapter Journal

I will: _____

_____

_____

I will: _____

_____

_____

I will: _____

_____

_____

I will: _____

_____

_____

Notes:

_____

_____

_____

_____

Chapter 11
Trainer's Guide

⬅ Look Back

Give everyone a chance to share, hear from others, and be held accountable. Focus on encouragement, celebration, and following through with assignments.

- **Have <u>everyone</u> report back on how they shared their story and followed through with what they said they would do since the last training.**
- Discuss how you have put into practice the things you have learned from the life of Jesus. Have you been reading/listening to the Gospels? What are you learning from the life of Jesus?
- Spend some time celebrating the victories you are experiencing and also praying for those who are struggling.

⬆ Look Up

Chapter 11 focuses on the story of the Church as recorded in the Book of Acts. It is critical that you focus on the following as you train through these chapters:

- How the disciples and early church faithfully carried out the mission Jesus gave them of making disciple makers.
- How persecution and suffering did not stop the mission of the early church, but only made the disciples and followers of Jesus bolder in their witness and proclamation of the Gospel.
- The importance of prayer to the early church and how the Holy Spirit guided every important decision they made.
- The fact that sharing the Gospel led to making disciple makers and ultimately to the planting of churches.
- **Remember to highlight the expected outcome and key principle!** Encourage memorization of key Scripture verses.
- **Hearing from God:** At the end of each chapter, allow for a time of silent prayer and reflection, specifically looking for what each person should do in response to God speaking to their heart.

Group Activity: Have everyone read through different sections of the Book of Acts (a few chapters each) and summarize the key events and teachings. Share your summary with the group and emphasize the practical teachings and spiritual principles that you can begin to apply in your daily life.

Model & Practice: Every trainer should spend time explaining the 8 key observations from the Book of Acts and how they apply those into their life and church.

Look Forward

Before moving on to the assignment for the week, ask the following questions:
- How is God speaking to your heart today?
- How is God calling you to greater obedience?
- What will you do today & this week in response to God's voice?

Assignment for this Chapter:
- Identify any unreached communities or peoples in your area. Begin praying for them and look for ways to share the Gospel with them this week.
- Spend extra time reading *Acts 5:17-42*. Take notes on how the disciples responded to persecution and how the suffering they endured did not stop them from proclaiming the name of Jesus.
- Write your I will statement(s) in the chapter journal.

Chapter 11
The Story of the Church

Expected Outcome: Every disciple maker will model the way they make disciples and plant churches after the example of the early church.

The Start of the Church *(Acts 1:1-11:30)*

The first 11 chapters of the Book of Acts cover nearly 15 years. During this time, the Holy Spirit came to the disciples and a great revival broke out in Jerusalem. This led to the first church being planted in Jerusalem. After suffering persecution from the religious leaders, many followers of Jesus fled Jerusalem for safer places to live. One of the men leading this great persecution was a religious leader named Saul. On his way to a city called Damascus, Saul had an encounter with Jesus that changed his life. As a result, Saul began to proclaim the Gospel to both Jews and Gentiles.

Until Saul was called by Jesus, the disciples focused mostly on preaching to the Jews, but eventually, they began to preach to the Gentiles (the non-Jewish people living in the region).

In this section, you will see how God empowers His people to obediently carry out the tasks of making disciples who make disciples. You will also read of God's amazing displays of faithfulness and love during times of hardship and suffering.

The Church Is Born in Jerusalem *(Acts 2:1-6:7)*

Before Jesus returned to Heaven, He commanded His followers to make disciples. In order to faithfully and effectively carry out Jesus' command, He told them to wait in Jerusalem until they were *"baptized with the Holy Spirit"* (*Acts 1:5*). Jesus said that when the Holy Spirit comes to them, the disciples would *"receive power and be [His] witnesses in*

Jerusalem and in all Judea and Samaria, and to the end of the earth" (Acts 1:8).

After the disciples watched Him ascend into Heaven *(Acts 1:12),* they returned to Jerusalem where they waited for what Jesus had promised: The Holy Spirit. About 50 days after the resurrection, 120 followers of Christ were gathered together in prayer. Read the incredible account of the arrival of the Holy Spirit.

"And suddenly there came a sound from heaven, as of a rushing mighty wind, and it filled the whole house where they were sitting. Then there appeared to them divided tongues, as of fire, and one sat upon each of them. And they were all filled with the Holy Spirit and began to speak with other tongues, as the Spirit gave them utterance" (Acts 2:2-4).

All who were in the upper room were filled with the Holy Spirit and started speaking in many different languages. Many Jews from around the world were in Jerusalem at the time and heard the works of God proclaimed in their own languages. Peter, who had denied knowing Jesus, stood up and preached about Jesus to the crowd. After his message, 3,000 people came to Christ and were immediately baptized. This amazing event (known as Pentecost) marks the beginning of the first church.

Group Discussion: Discuss a time in your life (in the past or right now) when you felt like God was asking you to wait for Him. Be honest about how you were feeling during this time. Encourage one another in prayer like the disciples did in the upper room in Jerusalem.

The Gospel Spreads in Jerusalem *(Acts 2:1-6:7)*

With the church newly established in Jerusalem, *"the Lord added to the church daily those who were being saved" (Acts 2:47).* The disciples whom Jesus first called began to make more disciples, teaching them about Jesus and performing great miracles before the people. After healing a man whose legs had been lame since birth, Peter and John were arrested for sharing the Gospel *(Acts 3:4-10)*.

Even though the religious leaders threatened them with violence and forbid the disciples from speaking Jesus' name to the people, the disciples prayed for greater boldness so that more people could be saved. Peter and John were arrested again and imprisoned by the religious leaders, but the Lord rescued them so they could continue to share the Gospel throughout Jerusalem *(Acts 5:19-20)*.

Empowered by the Holy Spirit, the apostles began to do many signs and wonders among the people; healing those afflicted by disabilities, disease, and demon possession *(Acts 5:12-16)*. Just as Jesus faced opposition from the religious leaders when He became popular with the people, so the Apostles and the early church faced intense persecution and suffering at the hands of the Jewish religious leaders.

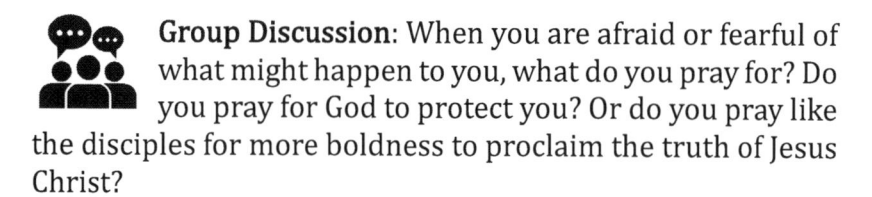

Group Discussion: When you are afraid or fearful of what might happen to you, what do you pray for? Do you pray for God to protect you? Or do you pray like the disciples for more boldness to proclaim the truth of Jesus Christ?

The Persecuted Church *(Acts 6:8-8:3)*

Though the church in Jerusalem enjoyed a time of growth and excitement, they also faced intense persecution including the first death of a follower of Jesus for sharing the Gospel. *"Full of faith and power" (Acts 6:8),* Stephen confronted the people and the religious leaders for their rejection of Jesus as the Messiah promised to Israel.

Stephen showed the Jews that Jesus was the promised Savior for the world, the One who would rescue them from sin and bring them back into relationship with God. Stephen's words greatly angered the people, and they forced him out of the city where they killed him.

Group Discussion: How does Stephen's example and testimony encourage you?

The Gospel Spreads beyond Jerusalem *(Acts 8:4-25)*

The Church in Jerusalem began to suffer for its testimony about Jesus and the threat of violence scattered many of the followers. Philip, one of the followers of Jesus who left Jerusalem, went to a nearby region called Samaria and began preaching Christ to the people there. Many believed after seeing him perform great miracles. The arrival of the Holy Spirit in Samaria marked the beginning of the next phase in Jesus' command to the disciples: to proclaim the Gospel not only to the Jews but to everyone! *(see Acts 1:8)*.

Christ Calls Saul *(Acts 9:1-31)*

There was great persecution of the church and its followers in Jerusalem. A Pharisee named Saul was given authority by the local religious leaders to travel from city to city, arrest believers, and have them killed *(Acts 9:1-2)*.

On his way to find more Christians to persecute, a bright light and loud sound knocked Saul off of his horse. Jesus revealed Himself to Saul, and he was blinded for three days. Saul (also called Paul), the most radical Jew, became a missionary to the non-Jewish people. (Anyone who is not a Jew is considered a Gentile.) When Saul began to follow Jesus and joined the early church, *"the churches throughout all Judea, Galilee, and Samaria had peace and were edified. And walking in the fear of the Lord and in the comfort of the Holy Spirit, they were multiplied" (Acts 9:31)*.

Although at one time he was a persecutor of Christians, Paul became one of the most influential Christians there has ever been. He established the church all over the Roman province and God used him to write much of the New Testament. Saul's joining in the mission of Christ would begin the final phase of Jesus' command to the disciples: to take the Gospel to the ends of the earth *(Acts 1:8)*.

Group Assignment: Write down a list of some names of people who you would never imagine following Jesus. Begin praying for those people and remind one another of Saul's miraculous conversion and God's ability to save anyone.

Peter Preaches Christ to the Gentiles *(Acts 9:32-11:18)*

Peter began traveling *"through all parts of the country" (Acts 9:32),* healing people and even bringing a woman back to life *(Acts 9:36-42)*. While staying in a town called Joppa, Peter received a vision from God that changed the direction of the early church.

At this point in the early church, the majority of the people who were being evangelized were Jews. The laws that the Jews followed during the time of Jesus and the early church forbid any Jew from associating with Gentiles (any non-Jewish person). This meant that Jews and Gentiles could not worship together or even eat together.

After receiving his vision from God, Peter understood that all people were made in God's image and were given access to God through faith in Jesus.

The Expansion of the Church *(Acts 12:1-20:38)*

Paul and the other disciples began to go on missionary journeys all throughout the Roman Empire to obey Jesus' command: to be Christ's witnesses to the ends of the earth *(Acts 1:8)*. During this time, Paul also trained other faithful men and women, like Timothy and Titus, to serve in the churches they planted.

Many churches were planted throughout the Roman Empire, and some were beginning to face various challenges and problems. This led the apostles to begin writing letters to the churches to correct where they had gone wrong and encourage them as they followed Jesus. The books of the New Testament that were likely written during this time include Galatians, 1 & 2 Thessalonians, and likely Matthew & Mark.

More Persecution *(Acts 12:1-24)*

Even though the church was again facing persecution, *"the word of God grew and multiplied" (Acts 12:24).* The believers were afraid for their lives, but they continued to preach Christ to everyone they met.

Key Principle: When we face persecution, we can trust that God will remain faithful.

Paul's First Missionary Journey *(Acts 13:1-14:28)*

After serving for more than a year in Antioch, the Holy Spirit led Paul and Barnabas to leave on a journey to preach the Gospel and plant churches in new territory. The strategy they adopted included the following: **Going to a new town, preaching the Gospel, planting a church with those who responded, and then training/appointing local leaders to lead the newly planted churches. They would then go to the next city and repeat the process.**

On their first missionary journey, Paul and Barnabas traveled more than 1,500 miles! On their journey, they confronted opponents to Christ *(Acts 13:6-7)* and proclaimed the Gospel to the most powerful people in the region *(Acts 13:4-12).*

After being rejected by the Jewish people in the region of Galatia *(Acts 13:46),* Paul and Barnabas preached to the Gentiles. The Gentiles received the Word of God with joy and excitement and became a foundational part of the early church throughout the region *(Acts 13:48).*

By the end of their first missionary journey, Paul was attacked and nearly stoned to death. Even though he suffered greatly, Paul saw God do amazing things because of his obedience and faithfulness to the Holy Spirit. Paul and Barnabas returned the same way they came, encouraging the new believers they had met along their journey.

> **Key Principle:** God can use any situation for His glory. Even those who persecute followers of Jesus can one day become disciples if we remain obedient to the leading of the Holy Spirit.

The Jerusalem Council *(Acts 15:1-35)*

Since the early church was still very young, the leaders of the church were still learning how to best lead and train new believers. At this point, the majority of the believers were former Jews who continued to obey the Jewish Law even though they were followers of Jesus. Since the Gentiles did not follow the Jewish law, some of the Jewish believers wanted the Gentiles to begin following certain religious and cultural practices like them. To deal with this issue and determine whether the Gentiles were required to follow the Law, the apostles and elders came together to decide.

Peter, Paul, and Barnabas told the entire group gathered in Jerusalem of the amazing things God had done among the Gentiles and how the Holy Spirit was poured out among them, too. Having seen for themselves the faithfulness of the Gentiles and their zeal for God, the leaders of the church concluded that the Gentiles would not be required to follow the Jewish Law. Instead, the Gentiles would only be required to not eat food dedicated to false gods or with blood. The Gentiles would also not commit any sexual immorality.

This decision was one of the most important events in the history of the early church. By not forcing the Gentiles to obey the Jewish Law, the leaders of the church were not imposing additional rules for the new believers. The church continued to grow and expand as Jews and Gentiles worshiped God together.

Group Discussion: When someone begins to follow Jesus, how can you best encourage them to start adopting habits and behaviors that are God-honoring?

Paul's Second Missionary Journey *(Acts 15:36-18:22)*

Before Paul and Barnabas were about to go on their next missionary journey, a disagreement arose between them concerning who they would bring with them. The disagreement became so severe that they ultimately decided to part ways and go on their own missionary journeys. Barnabas would sail west to the Island of Cyprus, while Paul went south through Syria.

On Paul's second missionary journey, he traveled more than 3000 miles with another disciple maker named Silas. As they traveled throughout the region, *"the churches were strengthened in the faith, and they increased in numbers daily" (Acts 16:5).* Along the way, Paul met and befriended a young disciple named Timothy. Timothy was born to a Greek father and a Jewish mother who followed Jesus *(Acts 16:1)*. Timothy had a good reputation in his community, and Paul invited Timothy to join him on the remainder of his missionary journey.

Traveling to some of the largest cities in the region, Paul had the opportunity to meet and witness to many different people. Paul told Jews and Greeks alike the Good News of Jesus Christ and His resurrection. He remained in a large city called Corinth for nearly two years until he returned to Antioch, waiting to be sent by the Spirit on another journey.

Paul's Third Missionary Journey *(Acts 18:23-19:41)*

On his final missionary journey, Paul traveled nearly 3,300 miles and visited many of the churches he had planted on the first two journeys. After encouraging the churches and believers along the way, Paul stopped in a large city called Ephesus. While in Ephesus, Paul healed the sick and demon possessed and brought the Gospel to people who had not yet heard the truth about Jesus Christ *(Acts 19:1-7)*. Paul sent his disciple Timothy and another believer named Erastus to Macedonia to encourage more of the believers there.

A great riot erupted in Ephesus because of Paul and the followers of Christ. Paul made a few trips to the surrounding cities before returning to Ephesus, but a final meeting with the church elders in Ephesus marked the conclusion of his final missionary journey.

The Future of the Church *(Acts 21:1-28:31)*

The last section of the Book of Acts concludes with the final years of the Apostle Paul's life. During this time, the majority of the New Testament was written, as many churches had been planted and the apostles were beginning to be martyred for the faith. Prior to the death of Paul around AD 68, every original disciple of Jesus except for John was killed for proclaiming the truth about Jesus.

Paul faced persecution during the last few years of his life, including accusations from the Jewish religious leaders in Jerusalem, beatings, and multiple imprisonments. All throughout his time in prison and under house arrest, Paul was writing. He wrote to the churches he had planted and the young men and women he discipled. He wrote encouragements, instructions, and corrections, helping them to better follow Jesus and train those they were discipling.

All throughout his life, from when Christ first called him on the road to Damascus until his execution, Paul remained faithful to what God called him to do. Paul is remembered as a great disciple making church planter. No matter the obstacle, Paul remained obedient and faithful to the leading of the Holy Spirit.

The Apostles Peter and John wrote their letters during this time as well. All of the parts of the New Testament written during this time are listed below:

- Ephesians
- Philippians
- Colossians
- Philemon
- Romans
- 1 & 2 Corinthians
- 1 & 2 Peter
- Luke/Acts
- 1 & 2 Timothy
- Titus
- Hebrews
- (Possibly) Mark
- Jude
- John
- 1, 2, & 3 John
- Revelation

Model & Practice: Lessons from the Early Church

Every trainer should memorize and practice sharing the 8 key observations from the Book of Acts and how they apply them in their life and church.

Key Observations from the Book of Acts

1. **The Apostle's Teaching**

Correct doctrine and clear biblical teaching empowered by the Holy Spirit are necessary for a healthy church to grow. The example throughout the Book of Acts is a constant balance between the leading of the Holy Spirit and alignment with the Holy Scriptures.

2. Fellowship, Evangelism, & Breaking of Bread

The early church loved and cared for one another. They took the mission of sharing the love of Christ with the world very seriously. They often shared meals and celebrated the Lord's Supper together.

3. Generosity and Service

The early church generously gave to people in need and served them well, both inside and outside the church. The church took it as their responsibility, according to their ability, to care for those in need. Consider what you and your church/fellowship can do to address the needs of your community. Write down some ideas below:

_____

_____

_____

4. Persecution

As a follower of Christ, we can expect persecution. We should never give up our faith, and when facing persecution, we must respond wisely and trust God. God uses persecution to form the character of Christ in His disciples. Consider the results of Stephen's death.

Stephen's death caused the church to scatter and move into other regions where the Gospel had never been preached. In the midst of persecution, remember to pray for the salvation of those who are persecuting others. Persecution could also be God moving you to another area to make new disciples.

5. **Disciple Making Leads to Church Planting**

Paul and Barnabas spent their time *"strengthening the souls of the disciples, encouraging them to continue in the faith. And when they had appointed elders for them in every church, with prayer and fasting they committed them to the Lord in whom they had believed" (Acts 14:22-23).* We must see how important it is to invest in others so they will become disciple makers and future leaders. Paul and Barnabas appointed multiple leaders (elders) who were Spirit-filled and godly in the churches they planted.

6. **All People Matter to God**

In *Acts 15*, it came to the attention of the early church leaders that the Jewish Christians were not accepting non-Jewish believers. The church decided that it was not right to keep anyone outside the family of God and that all people could be part of the church. **Are there any unreached communities or peoples in your area? Begin praying for them and look for ways that you may share the Gospel.**

7. **The Church Can Be Anywhere**

Paul always looked for people who were seeking God. He even witnessed to people who had gathered by a river to pray *(Acts 16:11-15)*. One of them, Lydia, responded to the Gospel and was baptized along with her household. After this, she opened her house for the ministry. From this story we learn of Lydia's generosity and how any house can be a place for the Kingdom of God to expand. Have you considered your house? Be bold in your faith.

Key Principle: Every believer is called to be a disciple, and every disciple is a disciple maker. Every disciple maker's home is a potential church, and every church is a potential training center.

8. Preaching the Gospel

Paul shared the Gospel with everyone, and even when he was jailed for his faith, he shared the Gospel with all who came to him, both Jews and Gentiles. As seen in the calling of Paul in *Acts 9:15*, God called Paul to proclaim the Gospel to all people. No matter what happened along Paul's journey, he preached the Gospel according to what Jesus instructed. God is faithful and expects the same from those who follow Him.

Assignment for this Chapter: Review each of the 8 key observations from the Book of Acts. Compare how your church measures up to each point. Identify opportunities for improvement and begin working towards a church that looks more like the one we read about in the New Testament.

1. _____

_____

_____

2. _____

_____

_____

3. _____

_____

_____

4. _____

_____

_____

5. _____

_____

_____

6. _____
_____
_____

7. _____
_____
_____

8. _____
_____
_____

Chapter Journal

I will: _____

_____

_____

I will: _____

_____

_____

I will: _____

_____

_____

I will: _____

_____

_____

Notes:

_____

_____

_____

_____

Chapter 12
Trainer's Guide

⬅ Look Back

Give everyone a chance to share, hear from others, and be held accountable. Focus on encouragement, celebration, and following through with assignments.
- **Have <u>everyone</u> report back on how they shared their story and followed through with what they said they would do since the last training.**
- Discuss how you have put into practice the things you have learned from the Story of the Church in Chapter 11.
- Have you reflected on the key observations from the Book of Acts? Did you identify opportunities for improvement? How have you begun working towards a church that looks more like the one we read about in the New Testament?
- Spend some time celebrating the victories you are experiencing and also praying for those who are struggling.

⬆ Look Up

Chapter 12 tells the history of the church to present day. It is critical that you focus on the following as you train through these chapters:
- Persecution and suffering did not stop the mission of the early church, but only made the disciples and followers of Jesus bolder in their witness and proclamation of the Gospel.
- The fact that sharing the Gospel led to making disciple makers and ultimately to the planting of churches.
- How God remained faithful to His people throughout history and how He comforted them in the midst of suffering and persecution.
- **Remember to highlight the expected outcome and key principle!** Encourage memorization of key Scripture verses.
- **Hearing from God:** At the end of each chapter, allow for a time of silent prayer and reflection, specifically looking for what each person should do in response to God speaking to their heart.

➡️ Look Forward

Before moving on to the assignment for the week, ask the following questions:
- How is God speaking to your heart today?
- How is God calling you to greater obedience?
- What will you do today & this week in response to God's voice?

Assignment for this Chapter:
- Spend intentional time in prayer this week for those who are currently facing any kind of persecution or suffering. Identify if there is anything you can do to serve or encourage someone you know facing challenges today.
- Write your I will statement(s) in the chapter journal.

Chapter 12
The Persecuted Church throughout History

Expected Outcome: As every disciple maker shares Jesus boldly, they will be prepared and encouraged to faithfully respond to suffering and persecution with perseverance.

The early church began the task that we now participate in as followers of Jesus. We continue to carry out the mission passed down from Jesus. Founded on the witness and example of the early church, we proclaim the Gospel to the ends of the earth, making disciples of every tribe, nation, and tongue.

The Church after the Book of Acts

The story of Christianity impacts every follower of Jesus Christ. The history of the Christian faith affects how we read and interpret the Bible. It influences how we worship God and why we endure suffering for the name of Jesus. It impacts how we view our government and those in authority. The church's history is our family history. Past Christians are our mothers and fathers in the faith.

The evil forces of this world are constantly at war with the church and will never stop opposing God's plan and His people. Fortunately for believers, we possess the stories, examples, and accounts of Christians who have gone before us in the faith. Their stories and amazing testimonies for the Gospel offer great encouragement and insight for modern-day followers of Jesus.

Group Discussion: Every culture and people have a history about how they came to where they are today. Discuss the history of your people and culture. How did you come to the place you are today?

When a child in your church asks, *"How could Jesus be God and still be like me?"* she is not asking a new question. She is dealing with an issue that, in AD 325, three hundred church leaders discussed in a little village named Nicaea, in the country of Turkey.

Even if you've never heard of Nicaea, what those leaders decided will influence the way you answer the child's question. Read a version of *the Nicene Creed below:*

We believe in one God, the Father, the Almighty maker of Heaven and Earth, of all that is seen and unseen. We believe in one Lord, Jesus Christ, the only Son of God, eternally begotten of the Father, God from God, Light from Light, true God from true God, begotten, not made, one in Being with the Father. Through him all things were made. For us and for our salvation he came down from Heaven by the power of the Holy Spirit, he was born of the Virgin Mary, and became man. For our sake he was crucified under Pontius Pilate; he suffered, died, and was buried. On the third day, he rose again in fulfillment of the Scriptures; he ascended into Heaven and is seated at the right hand of the Father. He will come again in glory to judge the living and the dead, and His Kingdom will have no end. We believe in the Holy Spirit, the Lord, the giver of Life, who proceeds from the Father and the Son. With the Father and the Son he is worshiped and glorified. He has spoken through the Prophets. We believe in one holy universal and apostolic Church. We acknowledge one baptism ... We look for the resurrection of the dead, and the life of the world to come. Amen.

Key Principle: We have *"so great a cloud of witnesses" (Hebrews 12:1-2),* not only in the Bible, but throughout the more than 2,000 years of the history of the church.

Consider the following timeline that summarizes the last 2,000 years of church history.

The Ancient Church (AD 33-313)
- The entire Bible was completed.
- The Gospel spread from Jerusalem to Judea and beyond.
- Churches met in houses and various places.
- Persecution was everywhere, and many followers of Jesus were killed for refusing to reject Jesus as their Lord and Savior.

The Christian Empire (AD 313-500)
- Rome accepted Christianity as the official religion.
- The church focused more on religion and rituals than true relationship with God.
- The church gained political influence, power, and prestige.

The Middle Ages (AD 500-1500)
- Islam grew rapidly.
- The Roman Catholic church became more powerful and centralized. They taught salvation by works and asceticism (self-mortification for purity).
- The Bible was translated in people's common languages in the 1300's.

The Protestant Reformation (AD 1500-1800)
- Key figures like Martin Luther and John Calvin opposed the Catholic church and taught salvation is by grace through faith alone.
- Importance was placed on the accuracy of Bible doctrines.
- An acceleration of missionary activity took place and the church began to spread across the world!

The Modern Era (AD 1800-Present)
- Man's reasoning begins to be seen as above or equal with God's. Everyone does what is right in his or her own mind.
- Modern and indigenous missionary movement spreads the Gospel to new and unreached areas.

Key Observations from Church History

1. **We know God better by seeing how He has worked in the past.** *Psalm 78:5-8* instructs us to tell our children, and all following generations about the works of God, so they will more confidently put their trust in Him. We know what God is like by seeing what He has done in previous generations.

2. **Church history covers doctrines and issues critical to our faith.** False teachers were common from the beginning of the church *(Acts 20:29-31; 2 Timothy 3:1-9)*. Paul and the other apostles fought numerous doctrinal battles to maintain the purity of the faith. The same is true throughout church history.

3. **Men and women have given their lives to defend the truths of the Word of God.** Even today, many attacks by false teachers continue. We can learn so much from how previous generations fought those battles and the conclusions they came to. Even more important, we must know what errors to avoid.
   - We must honor those who have faithfully lived before us. *Hebrews 11* tells of those who lived by faith and did great things in faithful service for God. But the record did not end there. Many other followers of Jesus have remained true to God and lived faithful lives.

Looking Forward: The End Times: (Revelation 20-22)

From the moment Adam and Eve sinned, God had a plan to restore His creation to the way He originally intended. He wants humans to have a place that is perfect with no sin and no pain. This return to a perfect place, where humanity can live in harmony with God, will come at the end of our time on earth.

Followers of Jesus today wait expectantly for the return of Jesus. Only God knows when Jesus will return to establish His Kingdom on earth (*Matthew 24:14*).

After the 1,000 years in which Jesus is reigning on the earth, Satan will be released. Having been given the authority and right to judge, Jesus will condemn Satan to destruction and throw him and his demons into an eternal lake of fire. All of the earth's unbelievers will also be judged and thrown into the fire. Christians will then enter the New Heaven and New Earth, where there will be peace for all of eternity, in the presence and perfect community of Almighty God and His people.

Persecution & Suffering

In *2 Timothy 3:12*, Paul explains that suffering and persecution are real issues that every Christian will face in their life. Scripture is filled with incredible stories and powerful teachings about how to handle persecution and suffering. Despite this, persecution is probably one of the least talked about aspects of discipleship. The Bible teaches that persecution and suffering grow us in our relationship with God and also instruct us in how to handle persecution and suffering well.

In Asia, there is a slogan about persecution: **If you imprison me, you free me to share the Gospel openly. If you put me in solitary confinement, you enable me to meditate on Scripture and to pray. If you beat me, you allow me to glorify God. If you seize my home or farm, you are freeing me to travel widely to spread the Gospel. If you kill me, you are sending me to glory.**

This statement makes it clear that no matter what the enemy does, we win. With this in mind, we can and should rejoice in our difficulties. Jesus did, Paul did, the disciples did. We can, too *(1 Peter 4:12-19; Romans 8:35-39)!*

There are many ways in which God uses or allows suffering and persecution to happen. Sometimes it is intended by God, and other times it is permitted by God though initiated by Satan. It is possible to suffer for the right reasons (as Jesus did) but also possible to suffer for the wrong reasons (poor decisions we make). In all times, we know God's grace is sufficient!

Responding to Trials and Persecutions

It is critical for us to respond to trials and persecution correctly because our response will determine whether the trial becomes a blessing or snare in our life.

- **Christ was persecuted.** Jesus endured intense suffering for each of us *(Hebrews 12:2-3; Luke 24:46-49)*. We can find hope and joy in the fact that He understands the pain we feel when we are persecuted for following Him. Followers of Jesus can also be comforted by knowing that Jesus is coming again to establish His Kingdom on earth.

- **We will be persecuted.** Jesus promised that the world would hate Christians for the message they proclaimed *(John 15:18-25)*. It is important to remember, however, that when the early church experienced persecution, the disciples and believers prayed for more boldness to share the Gospel *(Acts 4:17-31)*.

- **God intends everything for good.** Even in our sufferings, God helps us to endure. We can experience the good He intends for us when we respond well to persecution and suffering. *James 1:2-5* reveals some incredible truths about trials and how we should respond to them. **The Bible encourages us to face trials with joy because they produce endurance in us, which makes us mature and complete in faith.**

- **Serve as soldiers of Christ.** It's not a coincidence that Paul connects making disciples who make disciples with suffering as a soldier *(2 Timothy 2:3-4)*. We are in a spiritual battle, and like soldiers, we need to know what is expected of us. Soldiers are ready to make all sorts of sacrifices in order to live for something bigger than themselves. Likewise, we are called to serve as soldiers of the King of kings no matter the cost. **We live in order to bring glory to our King and to advance His Kingdom.**

- **Pray passionately, share boldly.** Once, the disciples were threatened and jailed. Immediately after they were released from jail, they gathered together with the believers to pray. They prayed passionately to God, thanking Him that He is in control and asked the Holy Spirit to empower them to speak His name **even more boldly** *(Acts 4:18-22, 24-31)*. They understood their mission to preach the Gospel and make disciples of the nations—no matter the cost! **Read *Acts 5:40-42.***

- **The battle belongs to the Lord.** This may mean that Christians are forced to witness violence against their church and their family. We protect our families and have the right to protect them, but we do not initiate violence. Read *2 Chronicles 20:15 and Romans 12:19.*

Key Principle: Jesus' disciples are called to immediate, radical, and costly obedience!

Recommendations for further reading:

- *Luke 9:23-25*
- *Acts 16:16-40*
- *Philippians 1:12*
- *Philippians 3:7-10*
- *2 Corinthians 6:3-10*
- *1 Thessalonians 1:6-10*
- *2 Thessalonians 1:4-6*
- *2 Corinthians 1:3-9*
- *2 Corinthians 4:7-11 & 16-18*
- *Romans 5:3-5*
- *Romans 8:16-18*
- *2 Corinthians 11:23-29*
- *1 Peter 4:12-14*

Assignment for this Chapter: Spend intentional time in prayer this week for those who are currently facing any kind of persecution or suffering. Identify if there is anything you can do to serve or encourage someone you know facing challenges today.

Continue sharing your story and God's story!

Chapter Journal

I will: _____

_____

_____

I will: _____

_____

_____

I will: _____

_____

_____

I will: _____

_____

_____

Notes:

_____

_____

_____

_____

Chapter 13
Trainer's Guide

⬅ Look Back

Give everyone a chance to share, hear from others, and be held accountable. Focus on encouragement, celebration, and following through with assignments.
- **Have <u>everyone</u> report back on how they shared their story and followed through with what they said they would do since the last training.**
- How has learning about persecution and suffering in the church impacted you? Have you experience it personally?
- Were you able to identify or pray for others facing difficulties? How did it go?
- Spend some time celebrating the victories you are experiencing and also praying for those who are struggling.

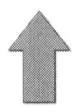

⬆ Look Up

Chapter 13 focuses on fulfilling the Great Commission. It is critical that you remember the following as you train through this chapter:
- We are not expected to fulfill the Great Commission in our own strength; we partner with Jesus and are empowered by the Holy Spirit to make disciples.
- Obedience to the Great Commission is the expectation and responsibility of every disciple of Jesus, not just pastors and church planters.
- Discipleship is an investment in the Kingdom of God. We may not immediately see the benefits of our time and effort, but the Kingdom of God will be advanced.
- **Remember to highlight the expected outcome and key principle!** Encourage memorization of key Scripture verses.
- **Hearing from God:** At the end of each chapter, allow for a time of silent prayer and reflection, specifically looking for what each person should do in response to God speaking to their heart.

Group Activity: Review together the current status and plans of reaching the unreached peoples and places around where you live. How is your progress? Is there something you could do as a group that maybe you cannot do as individuals?

Model & Practice: Plan a time for a special day of prayer and fasting for the people and places in your area that have yet to receive the Gospel.

Look Forward

Before moving on to the assignment for the week, ask the following questions:
- How is God speaking to your heart today?
- How is God calling you to greater obedience?
- What will you do today & this week in response to God's voice?

Assignment for this Chapter:
- Review your list of people you have been praying for daily. Are there people you need to add to the list? Pray for the boldness needed to continue sharing the Gospel daily.

Chapter 13
Fulfilling the Great Commission

Expected Outcome: Every disciple maker will be actively engaged in fulfilling the Great Commission.

The Great Commission has been given by our Lord Jesus Christ to every disciple *(Matthew 28:18-20)*. Let's take a fresh look at the Great Commission below.

Group Assignment: Read or listen to the following Great Commission verses and make notes about the unique parts of each passage.

Matthew 28: 18-20	
Mark 16:15	
Luke 24:44-49	
John 20:21	
Acts 1:8	

What is a Great Commission?
- Mission: a task to accomplish.
- Co-mission: a task to accomplish in partnership with someone else.
- Great Commission: the task of every disciple in

partnership with Jesus to make disciples of every people and place.

Jesus is our partner and chief commander in the *Great Commission.* He goes with us as we go to make disciples who make disciples. All authority in Heaven and Earth was given to Jesus—our partner in the Great Commission!

Let's look at each of these commands from Jesus.

1. **We Are Sent –** *John 20:21*

Jesus said to them again, "Peace to you! As the Father has sent Me, I also send you" (John 20:21)

Just as Jesus was sent into the world by God, He sends us to reach the world, too.

2. **To Everyone, Everywhere –** *Mark 16:15*

He said to them, "Go into all the world and preach the gospel to every creature" (Mark 16:15).

We are sent to share Christ with every man, woman, and child in the world. We all have different levels of influence in our lives made up of people we know, people we live nearby, our family and friends, and people we work with.

3. **With a Strategy –** *Matthew 28:18-20*

Jesus came and spoke to them, saying, "All authority has been given to Me in heaven and on earth. Go therefore and make disciples of all the nations, baptizing them in the name of the Father and of the Son and of the Holy Spirit, teaching them to observe all things that I have commanded you; and lo, I am with you always, even to the end of the age."

Jesus gives us a strategy for how we can accomplish the Great Commission. He commanded us to make disciples of all nations. *"Make disciples"* is the main focus in the Great Commission. There are three things that tell how we are to make disciples:

- *Going* – speaks of sharing the Gospel with people near and far. Loving, serving, and telling others how they can know Jesus is what we do as we go.
- *Baptizing* – baptism is how Christ-followers publicly declare their faith in Christ. They are now in relationship with others who can help them grow as a follower of Jesus. It is important that new believers follow Christ in baptism! Have you been baptized?
- *Teaching to Obey* – we are commanded to teach and model obedience to all of Jesus' commands.

4. **Telling a Message – *Luke 24:44-49***

He said to them, "These are the words which I spoke to you while I was still with you, that all things must be fulfilled which were written in the Law of Moses and the Prophets and the Psalms concerning Me." And He opened their understanding, that they might comprehend the Scriptures. Then He said to them, "Thus it is written, and thus it was necessary for the Christ to suffer and to rise from the dead the third day, and that repentance and remission of sins should be preached in His name to all nations, beginning at Jerusalem. And you are witnesses of these things. "Behold, I send the Promise of My Father upon you; but wait in the city of Jerusalem until you are clothed with power from on high" (Luke 24:44-49).

Jesus tells us to share the Gospel message with others. The **Gospel** means **"Good News."** The Gospel message is the death, burial, and resurrection of Christ.

- *"Nor is there salvation in any other, for there is no other name under heaven given among men by which*

> *we must be saved" (Acts 4:12).*
> - *"Now all things are of God, who has reconciled us to Himself through Jesus Christ, and has given us the ministry of reconciliation, that is, that God was in Christ reconciling the world to Himself, not imputing their trespasses to them, and has committed to us the word of reconciliation. Now then, we are ambassadors for Christ, as though God were pleading through us: we implore you on Christ's behalf, be reconciled to God" (2 Corinthians 5:18-20).*

5. **Equipped and Filled for the Task – *Acts 1:8***

"You will receive power when the Holy Spirit has come upon you, and you will be my witnesses in Jerusalem and in all Judea and Samaria, and to the end of the earth" (Acts 1:8).

Believers are empowered for this mission:
- The Holy Spirit empowers us to do the same works that Jesus did. The Spirit of God is the One who makes our witnessing powerful and effective.
- Every disciple maker and church planter must focus on sharing the Gospel. Jesus told his disciples that they would spread the Gospel in Jerusalem, Judea, Samaria, and the ends of the earth.

> 💡 **Key principle:** Making disciples and planting new churches in the power of the Holy Spirit is the biblical way to fulfill the Great Commission.

Model & Practice: Relying on the Holy Spirit

Plan a time for a special day of prayer and fasting for the people and places in your area that have yet to receive the Gospel. Fasting and prayer are spiritual disciplines that demonstrate our dependence on the Holy Spirit to bring the harvest.

We are called to be part of the Great Commission.

Understanding our identity in Christ reinforces who we are called to be and what we are called to do: *"Go and bear fruit that will last" (John 15:16).* Having the fullness of Jesus in us and working through us is critical to accomplishing what we are made to do. It is His fullness that overflows through us into the lives of others. The fruit of **being** a disciple is to **make** disciples! Our core mission is to be disciple making disciples.

If we take away the foundational mission of going and making disciples, we lose the major purpose of our calling!

"Discipleship brings our calling into focus and gives it meaning. *Discipleship and calling are inseparable.*" Discipleship is a never-ending process and God's plan for reaching the world. *The moment disciple making seems optional is the moment growth stops.*

Group Activity: Review together the current status and plans of reaching the unreached peoples and places around where you live. How is your progress? Is there something you could do as a group that maybe you cannot do as individuals?

In a discipling relationship, learning and development should be mutual. It is not just the teacher to the student. **What legacy do you want to leave behind? What do you want to be remembered for?**

We need to embrace the truth that our greatest impact will come not from our own accomplishments, but through the accomplishments of the people we disciple. In other words, *it is critical that we see our success through the success of others, not our own achievements.* To do that, we must take ownership of God's primary calling on our lives to make disciples as an overflow of our relationship with Jesus.

With this in mind, discuss the following questions:

- Are you intentionally investing your time and resources to ensure those you disciple are becoming more like Jesus?
- Do you see the success of those you are discipling as evidence of your own success? Or do you still focus on your own efforts and achievements?
- Have those you are discipling also begun discipling others?
- What specific behaviors and practices should you change to make disciples the way Jesus did?

Assignment for this Chapter: Have you finished reading or listening to the Gospel of John yet? Consider the questions below and identify what changes you need to make in your own life to be more like Christ. Don't forget to continue sharing your story and God's story!

As a disciple of Jesus, how should I live?

_____

_____

_____

Are the ways Jesus modeled making disciples present or missing from my life?

_____

_____

_____

What behaviors or values from the life of Jesus can be added to my life?

_____

_____

_____

The Great Commission and Church Planting

1. We are sent by the Father *(John 20:21)*
2. To everyone, everywhere *(Mark 16:15)*
3. With a strategy *(Matthew 28:18-20)*
4. Telling a message *(Luke 24:44-49)*
5. Equipped and filled for the task *(Acts 1:8)*

Chapter 14
Trainer's Guide

⬅ Look Back

Give everyone a chance to share, hear from others, and be held accountable. Focus on encouragement, celebration, and following through with assignments.
- **Have <u>everyone</u> report back on how they shared their story and followed through with what they said they would do since the last training.**
- Have you shared the truth about Jesus Christ with more people since you learned how Christians are empowered to fulfill the Great Commission?
- Did you share your story or God's story with anyone? How did they receive it? Spend some time celebrating the victories you are experiencing and also praying for those who are struggling.

⬆ Look Up

Chapter 14 focuses on the essentials of the Christian faith. It is critical that you remember the following as you train through this chapter:
- The essentials of our faith come directly from God's Word. Our beliefs are informed by our diligent study and application of Scripture. If you don't know the Bible, it will be difficult to know what to believe and how to live.
- People may have different perspectives depending on their culture and background. Strive for unity whenever possible.
- **Remember to highlight the expected outcome and key principle!** Encourage memorization of key Scripture verses.
- **Hearing from God:** At the end of each chapter, allow for a time of silent prayer and reflection, specifically looking for what each person should do in response to God speaking to their heart.

Group Activity: Assign one Essential Belief from the chapter to each person being trained. Have them look up the verses included in the description of each Essential Belief and discuss together why it is so important.

Model & Practice: Every trainer will demonstrate how their knowledge of Scripture affects their everyday life with Christ.

➡ Look Forward

Before moving on to the assignment for the week, ask the following questions:
- How is God speaking to your heart today?
- How is God calling you to greater obedience?
- What will you do today & this week in response to God's voice?

Assignments for this Chapter:
- After studying TTI's Statement of Faith and the Apostles' Creed, begin developing your own Statement of Faith based on what you have learned. As you read/listen to the Bible, note the verses and passages that support each of your essential beliefs. Remember to base everything you believe on Scripture! Don't forget to continue sharing your story and God's story!
- Write your I will statement(s) in the chapter journal.

Chapter 14
Essentials of the Faith

Expected Outcome: Every disciple maker will base their beliefs and worldview on a proper view of God and His Word by learning the essential beliefs of the Christian faith from God's Word.

The Christian discipline that studies God, His character, and His works that are revealed in the Bible is called *Theology*. **The goal of theology is to apply God's truth to life, live for God more consistently, love Him more deeply, and serve Him fully.**

What could be more exciting than to study about our wonderful God, who has saved us, and called us into His ministry? We are on a mission with Him to seek and save the lost!

Basics of Christian Theology
The basics of Christian theology are that *God exists* and that *He has spoken to us*. It is important to note that we begin this study with the belief that God exists, and we can know Him because He has spoken to us through His Word, the Bible. The basics of Christian theology can be divided into topics called doctrines or essentials of our faith.

What is Doctrine?
- Doctrine means *teaching*. **It is simply what the Bible teaches about a particular topic, principle, idea, etc.**
- Remember from Chapter 4, we learned that correct interpretation leads to deeper understanding and more meaningful application. All of this leads to developing right beliefs, and these right beliefs lead us to right living.
- A house built with blocks can illustrate the relationship between doctrine and theology. Doctrines can be seen as the building blocks or bricks used to

build the house, and theology is the house itself, for it is a more complete picture of God, His purposes, and what He is doing.

Why Should We Study Doctrine?
- We study doctrine in order to have the right biblical perspective about the meaning of life, the problems we face, and their possible solution (also called a worldview).
- The more fully we know God, the more passionate our worship of Him should be.
- The better we know God's character and personality, the stronger our relationship with God becomes.
- Studying doctrine will make our beliefs stronger about God's mission and help us to be more effective in sharing the Gospel with people in our community.

Key Principle: Approach God's Word with a humble heart and complete dependence on the guidance of the Holy Spirit, and He will always show us what to do.

"Now may the God of peace who brought up our Lord Jesus from the dead, that great Shepherd of the sheep, through the blood of the everlasting covenant, make you complete in every good work to do His will, working in you what is well pleasing in His sight, through Jesus Christ, to whom be glory forever and ever. Amen" (Hebrews 13:20-21).

Model & Practice: Knowledge Impacts Lifestyle
Every trainer will demonstrate how their knowledge of Scripture affects their everyday life with Christ.

Below you will see what TTI views as the essentials of the faith. Some call this a doctrinal statement or doctrinal position. We simply call it TTI's Statement of Faith, as it outlines the basics of what we believe. It is important to know what you believe and why you believe it! This must always be based on Scripture!

TTI Statement of Faith

What We Believe
- In essential beliefs — we have Unity.
  - *"There is one body and one Spirit... one Lord, one faith, one baptism, one God and Father of all" (Ephesians 4:4-6).*
- In non-essential beliefs — we have Liberty.
  - *"...Who are you to judge another's servant? To his own master he stands or falls... So then each of us shall give an account of himself to God... Do you have faith? Have it to yourself God" (Romans 14:1, 4, 12, 22).*
- In all our beliefs — we show Charity.
  - *"And though I have the gift of prophecy, and understand all mysteries and all knowledge, and though I have all faith, so that I could remove mountains, but have not love, I am nothing" (1 Corinthians 13:2).*

The Essentials We Believe:
The following is a list of what TTI considers to be the essential biblical beliefs. Removing any one of these items will lead towards false doctrine and teaching. They are all essential, foundational, and necessary!

- THE TRINITY (GODHEAD)
  - There is one God, co-existent, co-equal and co-eternal in three persons: Father, Son, and Holy Spirit *(Deuteronomy 6:4).* The Bible teaches that God is Triune (Trinity), which means God is one and in three persons: <u>God the Father, God the Son, and God the Holy Spirit.</u> This view of God is different than any other view of God in the world. Therefore, we believe that He is the foundation of all things. God experiences within the Trinity perfect love, joy, relationship, communication, etc.
- THE FATHER
  - The first person of the Trinity orders and directs all

things according to His own purpose and pleasure. He authored, created, and sustains all things in the universe without any means other than His own pure nature and power. By His grace, He involves Himself in the affairs of men, hears and answers prayer, and saves from sin and death all that come to Him through Jesus Christ *(Matthew 6:9; Ephesians 1:3; John 5:19)*.

- THE LORD JESUS CHRIST
  - He existed eternally as the second person of the Trinity. By His virgin birth, He came to earth as fully God and fully man, and lived a sinless life. He authored, created, and sustains all things in the universe without any means other than His own pure power. His death on the cross paid the penalty for man's sin, evidenced by His bodily resurrection from the dead. He physically ascended to the right hand of God the Father, and He will return in power and glory *(John 1:14; Colossians 1:16; 2:9; Acts 2:33)*.
- THE HOLY SPIRIT
  - He existed eternally as the third person of the Trinity. He convicts men of sins, regenerates, baptizes, indwells, instructs, and sets apart believers unto a holy life. We encourage all believers to seek a life of obedience to the leadership of the Holy Spirit. We believe this step is essential for empowering believers for victorious living and ministry through the gifts given by the Holy Spirit. The Holy Spirit is God *(Titus 3:5; Acts 1:8; 1 Corinthians 3:16)*.
- THE BIBLE
  - The Scriptures of the Old and New Testaments are the complete, inerrant (without error), divinely inspired, infallible (trustworthy) Word of God. The Bible is the supreme authority and guide for our Christian faith and living *(2 Peter 1:20; Hebrews 4:12)*. There are many ways we are to interact with God's Word: Hear *(2 Timothy 4:2)*, Read *(2 Timothy 3:16-17)*, Study *(2 Timothy 2:15)*, Memorize *(Psalm 119:11)*, Apply *(Ezra 7:10)*, Meditate *(Psalm 119)*, and Obey *(Joshua 1:8)*.

- THE NATURE OF MANKIND
  - Mankind was created in God's own image and likeness. He voluntarily fell into sin by personal disobedience to the will of God. As a result, apart from Jesus Christ, all people are spiritually dead or separated from God. The fall of humanity was a once-for-all historical fact. Its effect spread to all men, each of whom is born with a sinful nature and is in need of salvation *(Ephesians 2:1; Romans 3:10, 23-24).*
- THE NECESSITY OF SALVATION
  - Salvation (justification) is by grace, a gift of God not by works. Salvation (justification) includes repentance, a turning from one's own way to God's way. All who receive Jesus Christ are born again, regenerated (made new) by the Holy Spirit, and become the children of God. Our relationship with Christ is secure not by our actions but by the sustaining power and love of God. A changed life follows the work of God in a person's salvation (sanctification) *(Titus 2:11; 1 John 1:9; 1 Peter 2:2).*
- THE CHURCH
  - The church is the body of believers consisting of all born-again persons without respect to race, culture, age, or background. Directed by Jesus Christ and empowered by the Holy Spirit, the church is taking the Good News of salvation to the whole world. Our fellowship is inclusive rather than exclusive and stresses love for God and one another, the unity of all believers, and obedience to the Holy Spirit *(Ephesians 2:19-21; 3:10).*
- ABOUT ETERNITY
  - People were created to exist forever. We will either exist eternally separated from God by sin, or eternally with God through forgiveness and salvation. To be eternally separated from God is Hell. To be eternally in union with Him is Heaven. Heaven and Hell are real places of eternal existence *(John 3:16; 14:1-4; Romans 6:23; 8:17-18; Revelation 20:15).*

Group Activity: Assign one Essential Belief from the chapter to each person being trained. Have them look up the verses included in the description of each Essential Belief and discuss together why it is so important.

Consider this short simple statement below, which is known as the Apostles' Creed. It is widely accepted by the Bible-believing community around the world and is very easy to memorize.

The Apostles' Creed

1. I believe in God, the Father Almighty, Creator of Heaven and Earth.
2. I believe in Jesus Christ, His only Son, our Lord.
3. I believe He was conceived by the Holy Spirit and born of the Virgin Mary.
4. I believe He suffered under Pontius Pilate, was crucified, died and was buried.
5. I believe on the third day He rose again from the dead.
6. I believe He ascended into Heaven and is seated at the right hand of God the Father Almighty.
7. I believe from there He will come to judge the living and the dead.
8. I believe in the Holy Spirit, the Universal Church, the communion of saints, the forgiveness of sins, the resurrection of the body and life everlasting. Amen.

Recommendations for Further Study

These verses support the above statement of faith:
- *Genesis 1:1-31*
- *Matthew 1:18-25; Isaiah 9:6*
- *Luke 23:23-25; 24:1-8*
- *Luke 24:50-53*
- *1 Peter 4:1-6*
- *John 16:7-15*
- *John 1:1-4*
- *Mark 2:1-12*
- *John 11:23-27*

Assignment for this Chapter: Now that you have seen TTI's Statement of Faith and the Apostles' Creed above, begin developing your own personal statement of faith in light of all the things you are learning from God's Word. Remember to base everything you believe on Scripture! Don't forget to continue sharing your story and God's story!

My Personal Statement of Faith

Chapter Journal

I will: _____

_____

_____

I will: _____

_____

_____

I will: _____

_____

_____

I will: _____

_____

_____

Notes:

_____

_____

_____

_____

The Apostles' Creed

1. I believe in God, the Father Almighty
2. Creator of Heaven and Earth.
3. I believe in Jesus Christ, his only Son, our Lord
4. Who was conceived by the Holy Spirit
5. Born of the Virgin Mary.
6. He suffered under Pontius Pilate,
7. Was crucified
8. Died and was buried.
9. On the third day he rose again from the dead.
10. He ascended to Heaven
11. And is seated at the right hand of God the Father Almighty.
12. From there he will come to judge the living and the dead.
13. I believe in the Holy Spirit
14. The Universal Church
15. The communion of saints,
16. The forgiveness of sins,
17. The resurrection of the body,
18. And life everlasting.

* Memorize the statement above with the pictures on the next page as an easy way to tell and show what you believe.

The Apostles' Creed

Chapter 15
Trainer's Guide

⬅ Look Back

Give everyone a chance to share, hear from others, and be held accountable. Focus on encouragement, celebration, and following through with assignments.
- **Have <u>everyone</u> report back on how they shared their story and followed through with what they said they would do since the last training.**
- Were you able to create your own statement of faith? Continue to develop one if you have not and share it with those you are training. Encourage them to do the same!
- Spend some time celebrating the victories you are experiencing and also praying for those who are struggling.

⬆ Look Up

Chapter 15 focuses on defending your faith with confidence. It is critical that you remember the following as you train through this chapter:
- Being able to defend your faith and bear witness for Christ is commanded in Scripture *(1 Peter 3:15)*.
- There are more copies of the New Testament than any other ancient work of literature. The Bible is trustworthy!
- Jesus made many claims about Himself and the world that came true after His death and resurrection.
- The resurrection is the most important event in history because it was the moment that God made it possible for humanity to be reconciled to Himself.
- **Remember to highlight the expected outcome and key principle!** Encourage memorization of key Scripture verses.
- **Hearing from God:** At the end of each chapter, allow for a time of silent prayer and reflection, specifically looking for what each person should do in response to God speaking to their heart.

Group Activity: Have everyone share the different reasons they have heard from others for not wanting to follow Jesus. Take a few examples and discuss how you would respond to those objections or accusations. Pray for those you know who are resistant to the Gospel and ask the Holy Spirit to work in their lives.

Model & Practice: Every trainer should allow for any questions that people have and practically show from Scripture how they would defend their faith.

Assignments for this Chapter:
- Identify a group in your community that follows a different religion or worldview. Begin praying for these people and for opportunities to talk with them about Jesus. Don't forget to continue sharing your story and God's story!
- Write your I will statement(s) in the chapter journal.

Chapter 15
Defending Your Faith with Confidence

Expected Outcome: Every disciple maker will defend their faith with confidence based on the authority and accuracy of the Word of God.

It is important to know what you believe and live accordingly. Our knowledge of God should be applied in our lifestyle. Every disciple maker must be ready to give an honest and truthful answer for what they believe about God and why they believe it.

It is equally important to remember that defending our faith is a great opportunity to share our faith with others. The Apostle Peter wrote in his letter, *"Instead, you must worship Christ as Lord of your life and if someone asks about your Christian hope, always be ready to explain it"* (1 Peter 3:15). The goal is not to win arguments; our mission is to win souls. **Be firm in your faith, but humble in your sharing.**

Group Activity: Share the different reasons you have heard from others for why they do not follow Jesus. Take a few examples and discuss how you would respond to those objections or accusations. Pray for those you know who are resistant to the Gospel and ask the Holy Spirit to work in their lives.

Defending Your Faith from Evidence in the Bible

1. **We can trust the Bible:** The Bible is trustworthy and was written by eyewitnesses who told the truth *(John 20:30-31; 1 John 1:1-3)*.

2. **In the Bible, Jesus claimed to be God:** His followers, as well as His enemies, understood the claims He made *(John 1:1-14; 10:30-33; 14:6; Mark 2:5; Mark 14:61-64)*.

3. **Jesus proved His claim to be God by rising from the dead three days later:** He was seen by his disciples and over 500 people who confirmed this fact *(1 Corinthians 15:6).*

The Evidence for the Bible

The Gospels (Matthew, Mark, Luke, John) were written during Jesus' generation.

1. **The writers could not make up false stories:** The other eyewitnesses to the events in the Gospels would have rejected their claims if they were not true *(2 Peter 1:16).*
2. **Luke and the other Gospel writers were documenting history:** The Gospel writers wrote with the purpose of recording actual historical events *(Luke 1:1-4; John 20:30-31; 1 John 1:1-3).*
3. **The Gospels are consistent with each other:** Though there are some differences that exist between the Gospel accounts, these differences are minor and do not affect the essentials of the faith.
4. **Many of the biblical authors were martyred for their faith in Jesus:** As witnesses for Christ, they died because of their testimonies about Jesus. The disciples would not have been willing to die for a person or a cause that they did not believe to be true.
5. **Studies of ancient cities and archeological findings have confirmed the accuracy of Scripture:** The biblical descriptions of places, locations, and customs in the first century reflect those described in scientific studies done by historians and archaeologists.

The Evidence that Jesus Is God

Jesus clearly admits that He is the Son of God. *Yahweh, I AM,* was the personal name for God found in *Exodus 6.* This name was so precious to Jews that they would never even speak the word. But Jesus said it – and He said it about Himself. He is Yahweh *(John 10:30-33; Mark 2:5; Mark 14:61-64).*

1. **Jesus Was a Man of History:** Jesus was a historical person, a man who was born in Bethlehem, raised in Nazareth, and died in Jerusalem. Jesus was a descendent of Adam, Abraham, and King David *(Matthew 1; Luke 3:23-38)*.

2. **Jesus Claimed to Be God:** Read *John 10:30-33*. Jesus began by saying He and the Father are *"one."* This word means *"one in essence and nature."* He was saying, as He did in *John 14:9*, *"Whoever has seen me has seen the Father."* The Jews certainly understood what He meant because they accused Him of blasphemy and took up stones to kill Him.

The Evidence that Jesus Rose from the Dead

The resurrection of Jesus Christ is the most important event in history. The Apostle Paul admits, *"And if Christ has not been raised, your faith is useless ... we are of all people most to be pitied" (1 Corinthians 15:17, 19)*. Jesus did rise from the dead, so we have hope for the future, confidence in God's promises, and victory over sin *(1 Corinthians 15:50-58)*.

1. **Jesus really died on the cross:** There was no way anyone could have survived the torture that Jesus was put through by the Roman soldiers *(Luke 22:44)*.

2. **Jesus' body could not be stolen by His disciples:** A huge stone covered the tomb where Jesus was buried. It was so heavy that twenty men could not roll it away. There were trained soldiers guarding the tomb *(Matthew 27:65-66)*. The Jews who did not believe never argued that the tomb was empty, they only asked, *"What happened to the body?"*

3. **The disciples knew that Jesus had been resurrected:** Jesus appeared to John, to the twelve disciples, and, at one time, to 500 people *(1 Corinthians 15:3-8)*. The disciples

witnessed Jesus ascend into Heaven *(Acts 1:9)*, and the majority of disciples were killed for their faith and belief in Jesus.

> Key Principle: You can trust the Bible. In the Bible, Jesus claimed to be God. He proved it by rising from the dead.

Model & Practice: Defending Your Faith

Every trainer should allow for any questions that people have and practically show from Scripture how they would defend their faith.

To defend a subject, you must know it, be familiar with it, and have personally experienced it. One of the clearest descriptions of faith in the Bible is found in *Hebrews 11:1*, *"Now faith is the assurance of things hoped for, the conviction of things not seen."*

Every person, whether they are a follower of Jesus or not, has faith in something. When a person wakes in the morning, they expect the sun to rise. When they set foot outside their door, they have faith that the ground will support them. This type of earthly faith is not what is being described in *Hebrews 11:1*. The faith mentioned in *Hebrews 11:1* is not natural but supernatural. This faith is a gift from God, entrusted to followers of Jesus through the power of the Holy Spirit and God's Word. *"So faith comes from hearing, and hearing through the word of Christ" (Romans 10:17).*

Biblical Faith Includes:

1. **Trusting what the Bible says:** Since the Bible is the Word of God, we believe and trust it.
2. **Applying and obeying what the Bible says:** We obey the Word of God and let it guide and inform our lifestyle, worldview, and choices.

3. **Sharing what the Bible says with others:** We share what we know and believe with other people around us, everywhere. How we live is the best testimony we can show to the world.

By doing these three things, we are living by faith. This process is only possible through the power of the Holy Spirit. We pray fervently to the Holy Spirit to help us understand the Word of God, apply it to our own lives (internalize it), and, finally, share it with the people around us and in our community. This is *biblical faith*.

Biblical Faith Is Not:
- Memorizing Bible passages to keep in my head.
- Quoting Bible verses and explaining them.
- Singing gospel songs, shouting, and dancing in the church.
- Possessing what you declare and decree.
- Choosing passages in the Bible which support your own opinion.

Group discussion: Read *Hebrews 11:1* and discuss your understanding of faith in light of what biblical faith is and is not.

You can surely testify that since you've started sharing your faith correctly from Disciples Making Disciples – Level 1, you encounter many different types of people in your community. Some welcome you and receive the Word of God; some refuse to listen to you. Some people may try to convince you that you are wrong.

Sometimes, people who call themselves "Christians" try to prove false teachings using Bible verses taken out of their context. We live in a world where every person and every culture have their own way of seeing things, and their own opinions and beliefs. If we want to be effective in sharing the Good News, we must learn and understand other people's beliefs, cultures, and worldviews. Don't ever forget that we were in the world with our own worldviews before Jesus called us to His Kingdom.

That is why we have to defend our faith with love and patience, trusting the Holy Spirit to convince others that their incorrect beliefs and opinions may not be true or correct.

1 Peter 3:15-16: "But in your hearts honor Christ the Lord as holy, always being prepared to make a defense to anyone who asks you for a reason for the hope that is in you; yet do it with gentleness and respect, having a good conscience, so that, when you are slandered, those who revile your good behavior in Christ may be put to shame."

This passage is clear about our faith. When we believe and apply these words in our lives, then it will become a living testimony. Remember we are not called to defend God, He is Almighty. We are called to lift up Jesus and His Words, and He will draw men and women to Himself *(John 12:32).*

Here are some of the biblical truths people may attack as they try to argue against a biblical faith in God.

1. **The Bible**

Some may accuse the Bible of being full of errors and corrupted, or that it is not the Word of God. How can we tell them the truth concerning the Scriptures? One of the simple arguments we can present is that the Bible is a prophetic book. The Holy Spirit inspired more than 40 authors to write His Word. Some of them never met, lived in different areas, during different periods of time, but what they prophesied was accomplished and consistent.

Many of their prophecies concerned Jesus, the Son of God and the Messiah. Some of the prophecies took more than a thousand years before they were fulfilled. The Old Testament is full of prophecies about Jesus that were realized in the New

Testament. The entirety of the Bible, Old and New Testament, is about Jesus and His work.

Description of Prophecy	Old Testament Reference	New Testament Fulfillment
Virgin birth of Jesus the Son of God	*Genesis 3:15*	*Luke 1:35*
Place of His birth The Son of God is God	*Micah 5:2* *Isaiah 9:5*	*Luke 2:1-14*
Obedience of Christ	*Psalm 40:6-10*	*Hebrews 10:5-7*
The zeal of Christ	*Psalm 69:10*	*John 2:13-17*
Betrayal of Christ	*Psalm 41:10* *Psalm 55:12-14*	*Matthew 26:14-16, 21-25*
Suffering of Christ	*Psalm 22:2, 7-8* *Psalm 69:22* *Psalm 31:5* *Psalm 34:20* *Psalm 129:3*	*Matthew 27:34, 48* *Luke 23:46* *John 19:33-36*
Prayer for His enemies	*Psalm 109:4*	*Luke 23:34*
Raising of Christ	*Psalm 16:10* *Psalm 22:22*	*Acts 13:35* *John 20:17*

2. Jesus

Opponents to Christianity will often try to argue that **Jesus is not God.** Some may also argue that He is not the **Son of God.** One of the arguments they may suggest is that Jesus cannot be the Son of God because God didn't have a woman, nor was He married. As has been stated previously, if the Bible is the Word of God, we can trust what it says about Jesus.

Luke spent many years traveling with the Apostle Paul. After meticulous investigations, asking accurate questions of eyewitnesses, and inspired by the Holy Spirit, Luke recorded everything he heard and saw.

"Inasmuch as many have undertaken to compile a narrative of the things that have been accomplished among us, just as those who from the beginning were eyewitnesses and ministers of the word have delivered them to us, it seemed good to me also, having followed all things closely for some

time past, to write an orderly account for you, most excellent Theophilus, that you may have certainty concerning the things you have been taught."

Another teaching commonly attacked by opponents to Christianity is that Jesus did not claim to be God (Yahweh). Read *John 10:22-33:*

"At that time the Feast of Dedication took place at Jerusalem. It was winter, and Jesus was walking in the temple, in the colonnade of Solomon. The Jews gathered around him and said to him, 'How long will you keep us in suspense? If you are the Christ, tell us plainly.'

Jesus answered them, 'I told you, and you do not believe. The works that I do in My Father's name bear witness about me, but you do not believe because you are not among my sheep. My sheep hear my voice, and I know them, and they follow me. I give them eternal life, and they will never perish, and no one will snatch them out of my hand. My Father, who has given them to me, is greater than all, and no one is able to snatch them out of the Father's hand. I and the Father are one.'

The Jews picked up stones again to stone him. Jesus answered them, 'I have shown you many good works from the Father; for which of them are you going to stone me?' The Jews answered him, 'It is not for a good work that we are going to stone you but for blasphemy, because you, being a man, make yourself God.'"

Group Discussion: Discuss the words of both Jesus and the listeners in the crowd. How did their words show that Jesus claimed He was God?

3. **Salvation**

The Christian faith, based on the Bible, is the only one that believes and teaches salvation by grace through faith. All other world religions teach that salvation can be earned by works or good deeds. This is not what the Bible claims. The sacrifice of Jesus at the cross paid for all of the sins of humanity. No one, from eternity past until today, has been saved by anything other than the blood of Jesus.

Jesus came from Heaven to earth to do one thing: to reconcile the broken relationship between the Creator and humanity. With Jesus, it is all about our relationship with Him, not what we do or don't do, or our obedience to the rituals and traditions of religion. Salvation in Jesus is a free gift of eternal life. **Salvation is found in no one else, for there is no other name under heaven given to mankind by which we must be saved** *(Acts 4:12).*

Key Principle: By the power of the Holy Spirit, we declare the Word of God to those around us and ask the Spirit to give people eyes to see and ears to hear.

Assignment for this Chapter: Identify a group in your community that follows a different religion or worldview. Begin praying for these people and for opportunities to talk with them about Jesus. Don't forget to continue sharing your story and God's story!

Chapter Journal

I will: _____

_____

_____

I will: _____

_____

_____

I will: _____

_____

_____

I will: _____

_____

_____

Notes:

_____

_____

_____

_____

A Story to Tell When Defending Your Faith

1. In the beginning, there was God.
2. He created the heavens and the earth.
3. He created people to have a relationship with Him.
4. People turned away from God and made wrong choices.
5. These wrong choices separate us from God.
6. God planned to restore the relationship between Him and man.
7. God became a man named Jesus.
8. Jesus lived a perfect life.
9. He performed miracles and taught people about God.
10. Jesus died to take the punishment for all of our wrong choices.
11. Three days later, He rose from the dead.
12. After appearing to many, He returned to Heaven.
13. The Bible promises that if you confess with your mouth that Jesus is Lord and believe in your heart that God raised Him from the dead, you will be saved *(Romans 10:9)*.
14. Jesus promised to return. Those who believe in Him will spend eternity with Him.
15. Jesus' sacrifice and resurrection made a way for us to have a relationship with Him once again.
16. Anyone can have a friendship with God and receive the free gift of eternal life!

A Story to Tell When Defending Your Faith

Chapters 16-17
Trainer's Guide

⬅ Look Back

Give everyone a chance to share, hear from others, and be held accountable. Focus on encouragement, celebration, and following through with assignments.
- **Have <u>everyone</u> report back on how they shared their story and followed through with what they said they would do since the last training.**
- Did you have any conversations with people of other religious backgrounds or worldviews? How did it go? Pray together that the Holy Spirit convicts the heart of this person to seek the truth from the Bible.
- Spend some time celebrating the victories you are experiencing and also praying for those who are struggling.

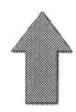

⬆ Look Up

Chapters 16-17 focus on understanding major world religions and spiritual warfare. It is critical that you remember the following as you train through this chapter:
- Belief in God is not dependent on how well you can argue; faith comes from God and only God can reach the lost.
- The goal of sharing Christ with those who follow other religions is not to show them why their beliefs are incorrect, but why Jesus and His truth claims are valid and trustworthy.
- We learn the basic beliefs of each world religion so that we understand others and can have more meaningful and intentional conversations.
- Some spiritual forces oppose Christ and the Church. If you are following God, expect spiritual warfare!
- Jesus has already won the victory against the evil spiritual forces in the world. We need to rely on Him and the empowering of the Holy Spirit.
- **Remember to highlight the expected outcome and key principle!** Encourage memorization of key Scripture verses.

- **Hearing from God:** At the end of each chapter, allow for a time of silent prayer and reflection, specifically looking for what each person should do in response to God speaking to their heart.

Group Discussion: Discuss what religions or beliefs you formerly followed and believed before coming to Christ. Which beliefs or practices were the most difficult to break away from or stop believing? Pray for those who are currently trapped in false religions and beliefs.

Model & Practice: It is important not to ignore or avoid those in our community who practice other religions. Every trainer will share one practical way they have developed a relationship with someone from another faith and help each person look to do the same.

Look Forward

Before moving on to the assignment for the week, ask the following questions:
- How is God speaking to your heart today?
- How is God calling you to greater obedience?
- What will you do today & this week in response to God's voice?

Assignments for these Chapters:
- Identify at least one person of another religion. Begin praying that God will reveal Himself to them and be faithful to share the love of Christ with them.
- Make a list of the sin areas in your life that you struggle with the most. These areas are likely the primary targets for the devil and the evil spiritual forces at work in the world. Share this list with someone you deeply trust and ask for their prayers and help in overcoming these sins, so that you can remain on guard against spiritual attacks. Don't forget to continue sharing your story and God's story!
- Write your I will statement(s) in the chapter journal.

Chapter 16
Understanding Major World Religions

Expected Outcome: Every disciple maker will intentionally develop God-honoring relationships with those who practice other religions.

A worldview is the way you see and understand the world. Every person and every culture has a worldview. Understanding what people believe and why they live the way they live is essential to effectively sharing Christ *(1 Peter 3:15-16).*

What is a religion? A religion is a belief in, or worship of, a higher power or deity, which usually results in a commitment of faith, acts of service, and a lifestyle of obedience.

If you can argue someone into believing in Christ, then someone else can probably argue them into believing in something or someone else. **Never forget that believing in God depends on faith, and faith is a gift from God.** There are thousands of false ideas and philosophies that compete for our attention. All of our efforts must focus on Jesus, what He has done, and why His truth claims are valid.

We should never give up praying for people who are resistant or opposed to the Christian faith. However, **we should never attempt to argue, force, or pressure someone into believing in Jesus.** We can provide evidence and give reasons for what we believe. Forceful conversions are not part of the Christian faith.

Model & Practice: Reaching Followers of Other Religions

It is important not to ignore or avoid those in our community who practice other religions. Every trainer will share one practical way they have developed a relationship with someone from another faith and help each person look to do the same.

Various Belief Systems

Animism: The belief that all objects and events in the universe have spiritual force and significance. Animism teaches people to fill voids in their life with personal spirit-beings and to achieve divine oneness with their gods. They attribute spiritual power to any object and believe that they can utilize the spiritual energy in these objects according to their own will.
- When sharing the love of Jesus with an Animist, focus on the **substitutional sacrifice of Jesus** on the cross for our sins. Focus on how He did this once and for all, offering eternal salvation and hope.

Atheism: There is no God or higher power.
- When sharing the love of Jesus with an Atheist, focus on the transformation Jesus has made in your own life.

Buddhism: Started by Siddhartha Gautama. Buddhism is a religion focused on suffering and its alleviation of a never-ending cycle of birth and rebirth. Buddhism's most important teaching includes the Four Noble Truths that form the pillar of Buddhism.

1. Life consists of suffering, which includes pain, misery, and sorrow.
2. Suffering comes from desiring those things that are impermanent.
3. Eliminating desire of those things that are impermanent is the way to free oneself from suffering.
4. Desire is removed by following the Eightfold Path: Right understanding; Right thinking; Right speech; Right action; Right livelihood; Right effort; Right awareness; Right meditation.

Holy Books – *Tripitaka,* the "three baskets" of teachings, include Buddha's teachings, rules for monks, and philosophical teachings. Others include the Lotus Sutra and

Perfection of Wisdom writings, along with the *Tripitaka* as Scripture.

- When sharing the love of Jesus with a Buddhist, focus on what we have in common, such as the danger of excess desire that leads to suffering, the value of prayer, compassion, and self-discipline. However, point out how Jesus does away with karma debt by paying for our sins with His death on the cross.

Hinduism: The belief in many gods and spiritual forces. There are some key beliefs that many profess:

1. **Karma** is the idea that every action leads to consequences in this life and the next. This continual cycle of death and rebirth is called reincarnation.

2. **Many Holy Books** – Hinduism uses a collection of prayers, hymns called *Vedas,* and the *Bhagavad-Gita,* among other epics.

- When sharing the love of Jesus with someone of the Hindu faith, encourage them with the fact that God is personal, and we can relate to Him without fear. God is caring and He loves all human beings, regardless of their background, community, sin, or struggles.

Islam: Islam means submission to Allah. Started by the Prophet Mohammad, following what he claimed to be revelations from the angel Gabriel and recorded in 114 chapters of the Quran (their holy book), Islam is built on five essential pillars:

1. Shahadah: "I bear witness that there is no God but Allah and that Mohammed is his messenger."
2. Salat: Praying 5 times every day.
3. Sawm: Fasting during annual Ramadan.
4. Zakat: Giving 2.5% of income to the poor.

5. <u>Hajj</u>: Journey to the holy city of Mecca at least once in a lifetime.

    - When sharing the love of Jesus with someone of the Islamic faith, do not be critical of the Prophet Mohammed, Allah, or the *Quran.* Focus on the love of God with prayer and faith. Understand that one can only receive salvation through the work of Jesus on the cross and the conviction of the Holy Spirit. Forgiveness of sins comes by grace through faith.

Key Point to Remember: While it is helpful to understand other religions, it is more important for you to know and live what you believe. Learn what the Scriptures say about God and about your relationship with Him. Faithful and loving obedience to God and His Word must always remain our top priority. **Our aim is never to diminish other faiths but to point people to Christ.**

Group Discussion: Discuss what religions or beliefs you formerly followed and believed before coming to Christ. Which beliefs or practices were the most difficult to break away from or stop believing? Pray for those who are currently far from the Lord.

Assignment for this Chapter: Identify at least one person of another religion. Begin praying that God will reveal Himself to them and be faithful to share the love of Christ with them.

Chapter Journal

I will: _____

_____

_____

I will: _____

_____

_____

I will: _____

_____

_____

I will: _____

_____

_____

Notes:

_____

_____

_____

_____

Chapter 17
Spiritual Warfare

Expected Outcome: Every disciple maker will be prepared for spiritual battle against the world, the devil, and their old human nature.

Preparing for Battle
When speaking and teaching about spiritual warfare, the disciple maker must be careful to find a balance between two extremes:

- Blaming evil spiritual forces for every problem they encounter.
- Completely rejecting the existence of evil spiritual forces.

Some people, especially those who live in cultures or people groups with many myths or folklore, believe and teach that demons are everywhere and are the cause of everything bad that happens. These teachers often believe that sickness, disease, unfortunate accidents, disorders of the brain, and many other negative things are all the result of demonic activity.

Others ignore the truth that the follower of Jesus has enemies who hate God and His people. These evil spiritual forces actively oppose the advancement of the Kingdom of God *(Ephesians 6:12)*, and it is their sole mission to stop the spread of the Gospel and distract disciples from following Jesus *(Matthew 13:19)*.

The goal of this chapter is to give a balanced perspective about spiritual warfare and a basic understanding of the evil spiritual forces that oppose God and His people. The disciple maker must be prepared for the battle, but they should not be afraid. **Jesus has won the victory and empowers believers to fight against the evil spiritual forces of this world.**

Before learning about the evil spiritual forces in this world, there are some important things for the disciple maker to know about spiritual warfare:

1. **We have victory; we are not fighting for the victory.** We claim the victory we already have through our Lord Jesus Christ. Through faith in Jesus' death and resurrection, we are *"delivered from the domain of darkness and transferred to the kingdom of [God's] beloved son" (Colossian 1:13)*. The attacks of the devil and his demons will stop when Christ returns to destroy them *(1 Corinthians 15:24-25)*.

2. **God is Ultimately in Control.** All of the evil spiritual forces that exist in this world are created beings. Even the devil is limited by what God allows. God is sovereign over all created things, including the evil spiritual forces that attack and harass His people *(Colossians 1:16-17)*.

3. **Spiritual warfare is fought by the power of the Holy Spirit.** The follower of Jesus is only able to withstand the attacks of evil spiritual forces by putting on the whole armor of God. The armor of God is the first line of defense against spiritual attacks *(Ephesians 6:10-20)*.

These three truths are essential for the disciple maker to understand in order to live a victorious Christian life, especially when experiencing spiritual warfare.

Group Discussion: In the Bible, there are examples of people who were in demonic bondage and facing spiritual attacks. Read and discuss *Matthew 4:23-24 & Luke 8:26-39*. Have you seen or experienced such things?

On several occasions, Jesus healed those who were suffering from demon possession *(Mark 9:25; Matthew 12:22; Luke 4:33-35)*. When Jesus sent His disciples out to the villages around Galilee *(Luke 10:1-23)*, He empowered them with authority to fight against the evil spiritual forces in the world. Through the power of Christ, the disciple maker today is also equipped to defend and fight against spiritual attacks in the name of Jesus. Remember, Jesus said, *"all authority in heaven and on earth has been given to me" (Matthew 28:18).* He also promised in *Acts 1:8* that *"you will receive power."*

Recognizing that evil spiritual forces are at work in this world is required for all Christ-followers. It is equally important to know what spiritual warfare can look like for the individual follower of Jesus, the Church, and the world.

How Spiritual Warfare Affects the Follower of Jesus

The primary way that spiritual warfare affects the individual is in the attempts made by the devil to separate people from God *(Mark 4:15)*. For the follower of Jesus, these spiritual attacks try to lead us away from the righteous path and calling God has given us *(1 Timothy 5:15)*. The follower of Christ may be deceived by the schemes and lies of the devil *(John 8:44)* or may be tempted to choose sin rather than righteousness *(1 Thessalonians 3:5).* **Remain strong and resist the temptations of the evil one!**

How Spiritual Warfare Affects the Church

Satan is the enemy of God and the Church. As an enemy of God, Satan actively works to disrupt the plans of God *(1 Peter 5:8-9)*. When problems arise in the Church, the devil and his demons rejoice at the lack of unity or love in the body of Christ. When the Church forgets or rejects its calling to share the Gospel and make disciples, the evil spiritual forces of the world see this as a victory against God. **We must remain** faithful to be who God has called us to be and do what He has empowered and entrusted us to do!

Spiritual warfare can also affect the Church when false teachers are able to mislead and distract followers of Jesus. In the churches that Paul planted, those who caused divisions *(Romans 16:17)* or imposed additional restrictions or laws on the believers are called *"evildoers" (Philippians 3:2)*. This is why unity in the essential beliefs of the faith is so important. Wherever the devil can gain a foothold, he will exploit, kill, and destroy *(John 10:10)*. **Make sure you are clear on the essential beliefs of the faith (pp. 142-144).** Anything not included in the essential beliefs are considered non-essential beliefs.

How Spiritual Warfare Affects the World

Even though God created everything in the world, Satan is described as the *"god of this world" (2 Corinthians 4:4)*. When the devil tempted Jesus in *Matthew 4:8-11*, he offered Jesus *"all the kingdoms of the world and their glory"* if Jesus would bow down and worship him. The idea that Satan could offer this in exchange for Jesus' worship of him assumes Satan has a hold over the cities and nations of the world. **This is not because Satan is more powerful than God but because God allows him to exercise greater influence in the world.** Satan oversees every part of this world that is broken and cursed by sin.

For this reason, spiritual warfare is especially present in the world, though many do not notice or acknowledge its influence and power. Not only does Satan blind people to the truth of the Gospel *(Matthew 13:19; 2 Corinthians 4:4)*, but he and his demons entice people to persecute the Church *(James 4:4; Luke 22:3-4)*. All who do not follow Jesus Christ as Lord are ultimately serving the *"god of this world"* and are vulnerable to the influence of the devil.

Group Assignment: Before continuing in the chapter, pause to pray for those undergoing any form of spiritual attack. As you pray, remind one another of God's provision of power through the Holy Spirit to all who follow Jesus.

Fighting the Battle

Not only do we fight against the world and its ruler (the devil), we are also in a daily battle against the old sin nature that still dwells within our body. This is called our flesh, the person we were before Jesus saved us and transformed our lives. Although we are saved through faith in Christ and empowered by the Holy Spirit to turn from sin, we still live in a sinful and broken world filled with many challenges and temptations *(Romans 7:29-8:1)*.

The ultimate plan God has for each one of His children is that they would be representatives of His Son Jesus to the world. It should be the goal and desire of every disciple maker to resemble Jesus in their words, thoughts, and actions. **Spending time with Jesus, loving Him, abiding in His love, and trying to live like Him are the greatest ways to resist the devil and live according to the power of the Holy Spirit.** The believer has security in Christ and the ability to reject the old sin nature. *"For you have died, and your life is hidden with Christ in God" (Colossians 3:3)*.

Despite his strengths and methods, Satan has one main weakness: he is a **creature**. Satan does not know everything and cannot read what is in our mind. He cannot be everywhere, all the time. As a creature, God the Creator is sovereign over him. The good news is Jesus, our Lord and King, came and destroyed his works. The devil was defeated on the cross and he knows that his time and rule on earth is limited.

Group Assignment: Read or listen to *Ephesians 6:12-18*. Try drawing a picture of the armor of God along with the functions of each piece. How does this help us in our daily spiritual battle?

Read the encouragement below from the Book of Jude and remember that through Christ and the empowering of the Holy Spirit, we have victory in spiritual warfare.

"Now to him who is able to keep you from stumbling and to present you blameless before the presence of his glory with great joy, to the only God, our Savior, through Jesus Christ our Lord, be glory, majesty, dominion, and authority, before all time and now and forever. Amen" (Jude 24-25).

Key Principle: We are not fighting for victory. Jesus has already acquired victory through His death and resurrection. For this reason, all the glory must be to Him and Him alone.

Assignment for this Chapter: Make a list of the sin areas in your life that you struggle with the most. These areas can become the primary targets for the devil and the evil spiritual forces at work in the world. Share this list with someone you deeply trust, and ask for their prayers and accountability in overcoming these sins so that you can remain on guard against spiritual attacks. **Don't forget to continue sharing your story and God's story!**

Chapter Journal

I will: _____

_____

_____

I will: _____

_____

_____

I will: _____

_____

_____

I will: _____

_____

_____

Notes:

_____

_____

_____

_____

Chapter 18
Trainer's Guide

⬅ Look Back

Give everyone a chance to share, hear from others, and be held accountable. Focus on encouragement, celebration, and following through with assignments.
- Have **everyone** report back on how they shared their story and followed through with what they said they would do since the last training.
- Which verses did you begin memorizing to defend against attacks and spiritual warfare? Discuss how God's Word encouraged and comforted you since the last training session.
- Did you make a list of the sins you struggle with the most? Have you found a prayer partner to help hold you accountable?
- Spend some time celebrating the victories you are experiencing and also praying for those who are struggling.

⬆ Look Up

Chapter 18 focuses on marriage and family. It is critical that you focus on the following as you train through this chapter:
- God designed marriage to encourage and empower both the husband and the wife.
- The home is the first place to begin making disciples.
- **Remember to highlight the expected outcome and key principle!** Encourage memorization of key Scripture verses.
- **Hearing from God:** At the end of each chapter, allow for a time of silent prayer and reflection, specifically looking for what each person should do in response to God speaking to their heart.

Group Activity: Have each person in the group identify the areas in which they want to improve as a husband, wife, and/or parent.

Model & Practice: Spouses and children are the first disciples the disciple maker should strive to reach and lead to Jesus. Every trainer will share how they practically invest in the lives of their spouse and children. Be sure to provide actual examples. Based on this, plan to spend intentional time with your spouse and children. Do something with each child one-on-one.

▶ Look Forward

Before moving on to the assignment for the week, ask the following questions:
- How is God speaking to your heart today?
- How is God calling you to greater obedience?
- What will you do today & this week in response to God's voice?

Assignment for this Chapter:
- Begin praying for your spouse and children every day. Ask God specifically to bless each of them, and that they would obey Jesus in their own lives. Don't forget to continue sharing your story and God's story!

Chapter 18
Marriage & Family

Expected Outcome: Every disciple maker will love their spouse and intentionally disciple their family to be more like Jesus each and every day.

Marriage: A Life Fully Shared

Marriage according to God's design is this: husband and wife are one flesh *(Genesis 2)*, equal in worth *(Galatians 3:28)*, complementing one another as God's image-bearer *(Genesis 1:27-28)* with the husband as the head, and the wife as the helper *(Ephesians 5)*.

The Role of the Husband
- Husbands are, first and foremost, servants of Christ. As a result, he submits to the Lordship of Jesus Christ.
- He leads by serving and understanding, just as Christ led His church *(Ephesians 5:23; 1 Peter 3:7)*.
- He loves his wife and his children unconditionally, just as Christ loved His church *(Ephesians 5:25; 6:4)*.

Questions for husbands to consider:

1. How does your wife feel served and understood by you? How does she feel cherished and loved by you? How can you show others how important she is to you?
2. Regularly ask your wife, "How can I better serve and understand you? How can I better cherish and love you?" Find a good time to ask your wife these things; listen and do not become defensive. Confess your failings and ask for forgiveness from her. Pray together for love, wisdom, and strength from God.

The Role of the Wife
- Wives are, first and foremost, servants of Christ. As a result, she submits to the Lordship of Jesus Christ.
- She helps her husband *(Genesis 2:18)*.
  - A helper is not to be considered a low or humiliating position. God is called the Helper of all disciples *(Hebrews 13:6)*. For a wife to help her husband means the wife fills in where the husband is lacking. The wife empowers and encourages her husband to fulfill his God-given role in the family and calling in the world.
- She submits to the leadership of her husband, just like the Church submits to Christ *(Ephesians 5:22-24)*.
  - Submission is not a humiliation but obedience to God's will. God the Father and God the Son are equal in being and dignity, but Jesus' role as the Son is to submit to the Father's will. Wives submit to husbands because they want to obey God.
- She respects her husband as the God-appointed authority for her and the family *(Ephesians 5:33)*.
  - In case of abuse of authority by husbands, wives are called to appeal to the Highest Authority (Christ) to intervene. Your husband is accountable to Christ. If a situation is dangerous for the wife and/or children, call the nearest authorities (father, church leaders, local leaders, or authorities) to intervene. Your husband is accountable to God, his family, the church, your community, and to the local authorities.

Questions for wives to consider:

1. How does your husband feel respected by your words and/or actions? Is there something you need to stop saying or doing? Try to show affirmation and give encouragement to your husband as often as possible.

2. What are the specific affirmations you can give to your husband (things you see in him that make you grateful to God) to encourage him in his relationship with Jesus, in his character growth, and in his work?
   - If you are unable to find any, you might have a wounded spirit. Ask for the Holy Spirit to help you share how you have been wounded specifically and release forgiveness for your husband for that specific wound.

Group Activity: Have each person in the group identify the areas in which they want to improve as a husband, wife, or parent.

The Role of Parenting: Making Disciples at Home

God's transformation begins in the heart. The best parenting strategy is focusing on the heart, not just focusing on bad behaviors. Behaviors are the fruit, but the heart is the root. Lasting change only happens when the heart is changed.

It is the primary role of parents to disciple their children by setting the example in the home and in their everyday life *(Proverbs 22:6; Deuteronomy 6:6-9)*. It is not the primary responsibility of the church planter, elder, or church to disciple children, but the family. Children are a blessing from God and He has entrusted parents to train them up as followers of Jesus.

Children are always watching or listening to their parents and will imitate both the positive and negative things their parents do. It is for this reason that parents should first focus on their own relationship with Jesus. Secondly, they should focus on their relationship with one another. If parents are unkind or unloving to one another, or are always fighting, this will affect the way the children respond to their instruction.

An Example Worth Imitating

In *Philippians 2:5-7*, the Apostle Paul wrote, *"Have this mind among yourselves, which is yours in Christ Jesus, who, though he was in the form of God, did not count equality with God a thing to be grasped, but emptied himself, by taking the form of a servant, being born in the likeness of men."*

The same humility Jesus showed when He willingly came to earth is what parents should try to have when raising their children. There is no better person for children to follow than Jesus.

Children are always observing and imitating their parents, for better or worse, and it is important that parents be a model worth imitating. Some of the characteristics and habits that parents should adopt to better show Christ to their children include:

- Love sincerely
- Confess sin
- Forgive quickly and frequently
- Follow the Holy Spirit
- Speak openly and honestly
- Be compassionate
- Be affirming and encouraging

Embracing these characteristics and habits will help parents model Jesus to their children. One of the habits that parents may feel uncomfortable doing is confessing their sins to their children. This requires great humility, but the confession of sin is an important practice that parents must model for their children *(James 5:16)*.

Group Discussion: How do you feel you are doing based on the above characteristics and habits?

Only by confessing our sins and our need of a Savior can we begin to follow Jesus as Lord. Model this for your children by confessing when you have sinned against them. Invite them to pray with you when you ask God for forgiveness. Ask your children to tell you how your sins against them made them feel, and ask for their forgiveness.

Another habit that parents must practice intentionally is forgiving their children when they sin. Most often, their sins will likely be related to disobedience or disrespect. When your child does something wrong, the best thing to do is to pause and pray.
- **Pray** and take a deep breath.
- **Resist** any motivation that is not godly.
- **Ask** the Holy Spirit how to respond.
- **Yield** to the Holy Spirit, and then respond.

Perhaps even more important than correcting sinful behavior in children is encouraging and affirming the behavior that brings glory to God. A kind and loving word from a parent will motivate the child to continue doing things that honor God and their parents. Be intentional and specific with your affirmation.

Group Discussion: What characteristics of Jesus do you model well for your children? Which do you need to practice and improve? Discuss with the rest of the group, and ask them to keep you accountable.

An Intentional and Intimate Relationship

While Jesus was often surrounded by crowds and onlookers, He spent intentional time with His disciples away from the large groups that followed Him. During this time, Jesus would teach His disciples *"the secret of the kingdom of God" (Mark 4:11),* bringing them into greater intimacy, friendship, and knowledge of Himself.

Whether you realize it or not, someone or something is influencing your children. The more time you spend intentionally investing in your relationship, the more it will grow. The better your relationship with your children, the greater your ability to influence and disciple them to follow Jesus.

Jesus knew that intentional time spent together was necessary for a healthy and thriving relationship. Consider the type of relationship you have with your own children. Do you prioritize time with your children over time with the crowds? Do you know what your children enjoy doing and what their dreams are for the future? Do you have more influence in their lives than their friends?

Do your children love you? Do your children know that you love them? If your children do not feel loved by you, they will likely not follow any example you are setting for them. One of the greatest hindrances to having a discipling relationship with your children is if they have a wounded spirit. Ask these questions to determine if your child has a wounded spirit:

- Does your child withdraw from you or avoid spending time with you?
- Does your child refuse to speak with you?
- Does your child disrespect or disobey you in public?

If your child regularly displays any of these behaviors, it is important for you to take the initiative to reach them and begin the healing process. Embrace the humility that Christ calls you to, and ask your children these three questions (remember to not become defensive, but receive their words gracefully):

- How can I be a better parent to you?
- How have I disappointed or hurt you?
- Will you forgive me for hurting and disappointing you?

One of the ways that parents can spend intentional time with their children is by including them in their ministry. Encourage your children to see their school, their friends, and the community as their own mission field. Let your children play a role in the church, showing them that their ministry and witness for Jesus is just as important as your own.

Group Discussion: Talk about your children with one another. Share their interests, goals, dreams, and what they enjoy. Share how you are praying for them daily.

Model & Practice: Discipling Your Family

Spouses and children are the first disciples the disciple maker should strive to reach and lead to Jesus. Every trainer will share how they practically invest in the lives of their spouse and children. Be sure to provide actual examples. Based on this, plan to spend intentional time with your spouse and children. Do something with each child one-on-one.

Preparing Your Children for the Future

The most important thing any parent can do for their child is to lead them to faith in Jesus. In order to successfully point their children to Jesus, parents must entrust their children to God and His Word. This means reading God's Word with them, praying with them regularly, and training them to follow Jesus. It is the parent's responsibility to help their children connect with God as only God is able to change your child's heart.

We can delegate the task of teaching our children to others, *but we cannot totally abstain from this responsibility.* Parents are instructed in *Deuteronomy 6:7* to teach their children the Word of God.

Your children are always learning and being influenced by someone. Shouldn't they be learning most from you? A well-known principle about discipling our children comes from *Proverbs 22:6: "Train up a child in the way he should go; even when he is old, he will not depart from it."*

An important part of training your children is through using discipline well. The purpose of discipline is that children may *persevere in growing into Christlikeness (James 1:2-3).* The motivation of discipline is love not anger *(Hebrews 12:11).*

It is important to teach your children that God has a unique vision for each one of them. Paul writes in *Ephesians 2:10, "we are [God's] workmanship, created in Christ Jesus for good works, which God prepared beforehand, that we should walk in them."* Celebrate God's "big-picture" vision for each one of them, even when it differs from your own or your other children. Have frequent discussions with your children about what God is doing in their lives and how He is leading them.

Group Discussion: In light of the information above, how well are you discipling your children? What behaviors and words do you need to change or stop in your life? What kinds of things do you need to begin doing in your home and family? Parenting well is only possible by the power of the Holy Spirit! Don't be afraid to talk openly about the challenges and struggles you feel as a parent.

Assignment for this Chapter: Begin praying these prayers for your children. If you do not have children, pray for the young people in your church. Pray one prayer each day of the month. Don't forget to continue sharing your story and God's story!

31 Prayers for Your Children

1. <u>Salvation:</u> Lord, let salvation spring up within my children, that they may obtain the salvation that is in Christ Jesus, with eternal glory *(Isaiah 45:8, 2 Timothy 2:10).*

2. <u>Growth in Grace:</u> I pray that my children may grow in the grace and knowledge of our Lord and Savior, Jesus Christ *(2 Peter 3:18).*

3. <u>Love:</u> Grant, Lord, that my children may learn to live a life of love, through the Spirit who dwells in them *(Galatians 5:25, Ephesians 5:2).*

4. <u>Honesty and Integrity:</u> May integrity and honesty be their virtue and their protection *(Psalm 25:21).*

5. <u>Self-control:</u> Father, help my children to be alert and self-controlled in all they do *(1 Thessalonians 5:6).*

6. <u>Love for God's Word:</u> May my children grow to find Your Word more precious than pure gold and sweeter than honey *(Psalm 19:10).*

7. <u>Justice:</u> God, help my children to love justice as You do and act justly in all they do *(Psalm 11:7, Micah 6:8).*

8. <u>Mercy:</u> May my children always be merciful, just as their Father is merciful *(Luke 6:36).*

9. <u>Respect (for self, others, authority):</u> Father, grant that my children may show proper respect to everyone, as your Word commands *(1 Peter 2:17).*

10. <u>Biblical self-esteem:</u> Help my children develop a strong self-esteem that is rooted in the realization that they are God's workmanship, created in Christ Jesus *(Ephesians 2:10).*

11. <u>Faithfulness:</u> Let love and faithfulness never leave my children but bind these virtues around their necks and write them on the tablet of their hearts *(Proverbs 3:3).*

12. <u>Courage:</u> May my children always be strong and courageous in their character and in their actions *(Deuteronomy 31:6).*

13. <u>Purity:</u> Create in them a pure heart, O God, and let that purity of heart be seen in their actions *(Psalm 51:10).*

14. <u>Kindness:</u> Lord, may my children always try to be kind to each other and to everyone else *(1 Thessalonians 5:15).*

15. <u>Generosity:</u> Grant that my children may be generous and willing to share, and so store up treasure for themselves as a firm foundation for the coming age *(1 Timothy 6:18-19).*

16. <u>Peace-loving:</u> Father, let my children make every effort to do what leads to peace *(Romans 14:19).*

17. <u>Joy:</u> May my children be filled with the joy given by the Holy Spirit *(1 Thessalonians 1:6).*

18. <u>Perseverance:</u> Lord, teach my children perseverance in all they do and help them to run with perseverance the race marked out for them *(Hebrews 12:1).*

19. <u>Humility:</u> God, please cultivate in my children the ability to show true humility towards all *(Titus 3:2).*

20. <u>Compassion:</u> Lord, please clothe my children with the virtue of compassion *(Colossians 3:12).*

21. <u>Responsibility:</u> Grant that my children may learn to take responsibility, for each one should carry his own load *(Galatians 6:5).*

22. <u>Contentment:</u> Father, teach my children the secret of being content in any and every situation, through Him who gives them strength *(Philippians 4:12-13).*

23. <u>Faith:</u> I pray that faith will find root and grow in my children's hearts, that by faith they may gain what has been promised to them *(Luke 17:5-6, Hebrews 11:1-40).*

24. <u>A Servant's Heart:</u> God, please help my children develop a servants' heart, that by faith they may serve

wholeheartedly, as if they were serving the Lord, not men *(Ephesians 6:7)*.

25. <u>Hope:</u> May the God of hope grant that my children may overflow with hope by the power of the Holy Spirit *(Romans 15:13)*.

26. <u>Willingness and ability to work:</u> Teach my children, Lord, to value work and to work at it with all their heart, as working for the Lord, not for men *(Colossians 3:23)*.

27. <u>Passion for God:</u> Lord, please create in my children a soul that pursues You, one that seeks passionately after You *(Psalm 63:8)*.

28. <u>Self-discipline:</u> Father, I pray that my children may acquire a disciplined and prudent life, doing what is right and just and fair *(Proverbs 1:3)*.

29. <u>Prayerfulness:</u> Grant, Lord, that my children's lives may be marked by prayerfulness, that they may learn to pray in the Spirit on all occasions with all kinds of prayers and requests *(Ephesians 6:18)*.

30. <u>Gratitude:</u> Help my children to live lives that are overflowing with thankfulness to God, the Father, for everything, in the name of our Lord Jesus Christ *(Ephesians 5:20, Colossians 2:7)*.

31. <u>A heart of missions:</u> Lord please help my children to develop a desire to see Your glory declared among the nations, Your marvelous deeds among all peoples *(Psalm. 96:3)*.

Further Study on Parenting

Train your children in the biblical truths of their identity, their world, their friends, and their family in order to face the trials and temptations of living in this challenging world.

Concerning their identity, tell your child:
- You are unique *(Psalms 139:14)*.
- You are God's sons and daughters *(1 John 3:1-2)*.
- You are blessed *(Romans 8:28-29; 1 Thessalonian 5:18)*, with parents, with God-given sexuality *(Genesis 1:27)*, with physicality, and with language and ethnicity.
- You are Christlike *(Romans 8:29)*.
- You are enabled and empowered by God *(Philippians 4:13)*.

Concerning the world, tell your child:
- They are different than the world, and not to be like those in the world *(Romans 12:1-2)*.
  - Therefore, be committed to purity, even in the midst of an impure world *(1 Corinthians 6:9-11; 2 Timothy 2:22)*.
- To be filled with the Holy Spirit, in a world full of desires and addictions *(Ephesians 5:18)*.
- To spend time and seize opportunities to grow in wisdom, in the midst of a time-wasting world *(Ephesians 5:15-17)*.
- To live by faith to please God, not comfortable lives to please man *(2 Corinthians 5:9-10)*.
- To know that this momentary world is short, and eternity is long. Therefore, not to love the things of the world *(1 John 2:15)*.
- To be fruitful and impactful in the world, for the glory of God *(Matthew 5:13-14, 16)*!

Concerning their friends, teach your child:
- The blessing of true friendship *(Proverbs 13:20; 22:24-25)*.
- The freedom of waiting, especially in delaying intimate relationships. When we do wait, there is freedom from distraction, unnecessary wounds, isolation, hindrances to pursue God's will and develop talent, and the consequences of immorality.
- Teach them to consider how their future spouse will partner with them in the spreading of the Gospel.

Concerning their family, teach your child:
- To respect one another as they would like to be respected *(Matthew 7:12)*.
- To forgive one another *(Ephesians 4:31-32)*.
- To give and invest in one another *(Philippians 2:4; Matthew 6:21)*.
- To be wise in stewarding their privileges *(Romans 14:13)*.

Entrusting Our Children to God and His Word

Who God is, based on Scripture:
- Sovereign *(Psalm 135:6)*
- All-Knowing *(Psalm 139:2-4)*
- Good *(Psalm 136:1; Romans 8:28)*
- Loving *(Romans 5:8)*
- The Giver of Gifts *(Hebrews 11:6)*
- The King and the Judge *(Romans 14:11-12)*

Questions to consider:

1. What are the truths that your children need to know about God?

_____

_____

_____

2. What will you do to help your children connect with God?

_____

_____

_____

3. How do you develop the habit of prayer and reading Scripture at your home?

_____

_____

_____

4. Do your children believe in the authority of Scripture?

5. What do you need to stop saying and doing?

6. What do you need to start saying and doing?

7. Pray to God, entrust your children to Him, bringing their names one by one before the Lord.

Your Investment

Congratulations! You have completed the written training for Disciples Making Disciples - Level 3. By now, you are a disciple who makes disciples. We pray you have started at least one or more multiplying churches that will impact your town, city, and region for Jesus Christ.

You have invested a significant portion of your time, energy, gifts and focus to become a stronger follower of Jesus Christ and lead others with you for the sake of His Gospel. It is our honor to work in partnership with you and watch you grow as a disciple of Jesus Christ who starts churches for His glory.

This manual was designed to encourage you to:

1. Live in a love relationship with God.
2. Grow continually as a Christlike leader.
3. Reproduce disciple making leaders who are planting multiplying churches.

Success is always measured by spiritual reproduction of maturing disciple makers.

You have received well-rounded training. God now calls you to multiply even more what you have learned and invest your life; investing in others by making disciples who make disciples. You make disciples by going, by reaching out to those without Jesus Christ as their personal Savior and God, winning them to Christ under the power of the Holy Spirit and then baptizing them. At that point their new life starts by you and others teaching them all that Jesus commanded in His Word *(Matthew 28:18-20)*. That will take a lifetime…a lifetime where He will be with you always.

Let's worship the King whom this Book is dedicated to, the King of kings, Jesus Christ. In Heaven we will be together with you to celebrate His name, His activity and His power. We are proud of you. We love you! Until we all meet on this day:

"After this I looked, and behold, a great multitude that no one could number, from every nation, from all tribes and peoples and languages, standing before the throne and before the Lamb, clothed in white robes, with palm branches in their hands, and crying out with a loud voice, 'Salvation belongs to our God who sits on the throne, and to the Lamb!' And all the angels were standing around the throne and around the elders and the four living creatures, and they fell on their faces before the throne and worshiped God, saying, 'Amen! Blessing and glory and wisdom and thanksgiving and honor and power and might be to our God forever and ever! Amen'" (Revelation 7:9-12).

APPENDIX
Bible Reading Guides

Old Testament Reading Guide:
Every day, listen or read one chapter from the Old Testament. You will complete the full Old Testament in 3 years because it has 929 chapters. After each chapter you read, cross out the number for that chapter.

New Testament Reading Guide:
Every day, listen or read one chapter from the New Testament. You will complete the full New Testament in only 260 days because it has only 260 chapters. After each chapter you read, cross out the number for that chapter.

	The Old Testament
Genesis	1 2 3 4 5 6 7 8 9 10 11 12 13 14 15 16 17 18 19 20 21 22 23 24 25 26 27 28 29 30 31 32 33 34 35 36 37 38 39 40 41 42 43 44 45 46 47 48 49 50
Exodus	1 2 3 4 5 6 7 8 9 10 11 12 13 14 15 16 17 18 19 20 21 22 23 24 25 26 27 28 29 30 31 32 33 34 35 36 37 38 39 40
Leviticus	1 2 3 4 5 6 7 8 9 10 11 12 13 14 15 16 17 18 19 20 21 22 23 24 25 26 27
Numbers	1 2 3 4 5 6 7 8 9 10 11 12 13 14 15 16 17 18 19 20 21 22 23 24 25 26 27 28 29 30 31 32 33 34 35 36
Deuteronomy	1 2 3 4 5 6 7 8 9 10 11 12 13 14 15 16 17 18 19 20 21 22 23 24 25 26 27 28 29 30 31 32 33 34
Joshua	1 2 3 4 5 6 7 8 9 10 11 12 13 14 15 16 17 18 19 20 21 22 23 24
Judges	1 2 3 4 5 6 7 8 9 10 11 12 13 14 15 16 17 18 19 20 21
Ruth	1 2 3 4
1 Samuel	1 2 3 4 5 6 7 8 9 10 11 12 13 14 15 16 17 18 19 20 21 22 23 24 25 26 27 28 29 30 31
2 Samuel	1 2 3 4 5 6 7 8 9 10 11 12 13 14 15 16 17 18 19 20 21 22 23 24
1 Kings	1 2 3 4 5 6 7 8 9 10 11 12 13 14 15 16 17 18 19 20 21 22
2 Kings	1 2 3 4 5 6 7 8 9 10 11 12 13 14 15 16 17 18 19 20 21 22 23 24 25
1 Chronicles	1 2 3 4 5 6 7 8 9 10 11 12 13 14 15 16 17 18 19 20 21 22 23 24 25 26 27 28 29
2 Chronicles	1 2 3 4 5 6 7 8 9 10 11 12 13 14 15 16 17 18 19 20 21 22 23 24 25 26 27 28 29 30 31 32 33 34 35 36
Ezra	1 2 3 4 5 6 7 8 9 10

Book	Chapters
Nehemiah	1 2 3 4 5 6 7 8 9 10 11 12 13
Esther	1 2 3 4 5 6 7 8 9 10
Job	1 2 3 4 5 6 7 8 9 10 11 12 13 14 15 16 17 18 19 20 21 22 23 24 25 26 27 28 29 30 31 32 33 34 35 36 37 38 39 40 41 42
Psalms	1 2 3 4 5 6 7 8 9 10 11 12 13 14 15 16 17 18 19 20 21 22 23 24 25 26 27 28 29 30 31 32 33 34 35 36 37 38 39 40 41 42 43 44 45 46 47 48 49 50 51 52 53 54 55 56 57 58 59 60 61 62 63 64 65 66 67 68 69 70 71 72 73 74 75 76 77 78 79 80 81 82 83 84 85 86 87 88 89 90 91 92 93 94 95 96 97 98 99 100 101 102 103 104 105 106 107 108 109 110 111 112 113 114 115 116 117 118 119 120 121 122 123 124 125 126 127 128 129 130 131 132 133 134 135 136 137 138 139 140 141 142 143 144 145 146 147 148 149 150
Proverbs	1 2 3 4 5 6 7 8 9 10 11 12 13 14 15 16 17 18 19 20 21 22 23 24 25 26 27 28 29 30 31
Ecclesiastes	1 2 3 4 5 6 7 8 9 10 11 12
Song of Songs	1 2 3 4 5 6 7 8
Isaiah	1 2 3 4 5 6 7 8 9 10 11 12 13 14 15 16 17 18 19 20 21 22 23 24 25 26 27 28 29 30 31 32 33 34 35 36 37 38 39 40 41 42 43 44 45 46 47 48 49 50 51 52 53 54 55 56 57 58 59 60 61 62 63 64 65 66
Jeremiah	1 2 3 4 5 6 7 8 9 10 11 12 13 14 15 16 17 18 19 20 21 22 23 24 25 26 27 28 29 30 31 32 33 34 35 36 37 38 39 40 41 42 43 44 45 46 47 48 49 50 51 52
Lamentations	1 2 3 4 5
Ezekiel	1 2 3 4 5 6 7 8 9 10 11 12 13 14 15 16 17 18 19 20 21 22 23 24 25 26 27 28 29 30 31 32 33 34 35 36 37 38 39 40 41 42 43 44 45 46 47 48
Daniel	1 2 3 4 5 6 7 8 9 10 11 12
Hosea	1 2 3 4 5 6 7 8 9 10 11 12 13 14

Joel	1 2 3
Amos	1 2 3 4 5 6 7 8 9
Obadiah	1
Jonah	1 2 3 4
Micah	1 2 3 4 5 6 7
Nahum	1 2 3
Habakkuk	1 2 3
Zephaniah	1 2 3
Haggai	1 2
Zechariah	1 2 3 4 5 6 7 8 9 10 11 12 13 14
Malachi	1 2 3 4

	The New Testament
Matthew	1 2 3 4 5 6 7 8 9 10 11 12 13 14 15 16 17 18 19 20 21 22 23 24 25 26 27 28
Mark	1 2 3 4 5 6 7 8 9 10 11 12 13 14 15 16
Luke	1 2 3 4 5 6 7 8 9 10 11 12 13 14 15 16 17 18 19 20 21 22 23 24
John	1 2 3 4 5 6 7 8 9 10 11 12 13 14 15 16 17 18 19 20 21
Acts	1 2 3 4 5 6 7 8 9 10 11 12 13 14 15 16 17 18 19 20 21 22 23 24 25 26 27 28
Romans	1 2 3 4 5 6 7 8 9 10 11 12 13 14 15 16
1 Corinthians	1 2 3 4 5 6 7 8 9 10 11 12 13 14 15 16
2 Corinthians	1 2 3 4 5 6 7 8 9 10 11 12 13
Galatians	1 2 3 4 5 6
Ephesians	1 2 3 4 5 6
Philippians	1 2 3 4
Colossians	1 2 3 4
1 Thessalonians	1 2 3 4 5
2 Thessalonians	1 2 3
1 Timothy	1 2 3 4 5 6
2 Timothy	1 2 3 4
Titus	1 2 3
Philemon	1
Hebrews	1 2 3 4 5 6 7 8 9 10 11 12 13
James	1 2 3 4 5
1 Peter	1 2 3 4 5
2 Peter	1 2 3
1 John	1 2 3 4 5
2 John	1
3 John	1
Jude	1
Revelation	1 2 3 4 5 6 7 8 9 10 11 12 13 14 15 16 17 18 19 20 21 22

Made in the USA
Middletown, DE
28 November 2022